What if?

What Would Happen if...?

DR. KNUT OLSEN

iUniverse LLC
Bloomington

What if?
What Would Happen if...?

iUniverse books may be ordered through booksellers or by contacting:

iUniverse LLC
1663 Liberty Drive
Bloomington, IN 47403
www.iuniverse.com
1-800-Authors (1-800-288-4677)

ISBN: 978-1-4917-0527-8 (sc)
ISBN: 978-1-4917-0528-5 (hc)
ISBN: 978-1-4917-1186-6 (e)

Library of Congress Control Number: 2013915351

Printed in the United States of America.

iUniverse rev. date: 03/24/2014

Contents

Introduction

During the month of October 2012, 55,600,000 people searched Google for the words *'what if'* in English. If we were to take all languages into account, there were probably considerably more than 100 million people who searched for the phrase. But what did they expect to find? There is no way of knowing the answer to 'what if', but this book will throw up a multitude of links for humorous stories, history, science, and sex, in addition to some serious questions, such as the following:

What if Adam had been gay?

What if the French were not so bloody arrogant?

What if you woke up one morning and noticed that you were dead?

What if you survived an abortion?

What if you had a few hours more each day?

What if you had to go on holiday with your ex for one month?

What if everybody in the United States flushed the toilet at the same time?

What if we did not have 'zero'?

What if you could call God?

Curiosity is a very human trait. Have *you* ever thought about how you might be affected by a certain event? What would or could have happened if? What if . . . ? Think about it.

We are surrounded by what-ifs, and some of them are so serious that you might not be prepared to consider them. While some are unthinkable or unrealistic, many of them are fun.

This book is not intended to be a work of science; on the contrary, the writer hopes to raise a smile or two.

Sometimes, I give answers to the what-if, and other times, I do not. You might agree or disagree, but consider and enjoy your own answers. Although I provide some references, do not take them too seriously.

Share with friends, colleagues, children, parents, neighbours, at parties and on social networks like Facebook and Twitter. Have fun, think about the questions, and figure out your own answers.

Whether you agree or disagree, whether you love it or hate it, or if you have other what-ifs you want to share, go to *www.whatif.uk.com* and post your comments.

Although most of the content in the book is for fun, there are some quite seriously what-ifs.

Think about it.

Abuse

What if you were bugged by the government?

It is very likely you are.

What if the government is spying on us?

It happens all the time. George Orwell's fictional *1984*, Big Brother is watching you, has come true.

What if we knew how much the government knew about each of us and how much information they keep?

What if the government was honest and admitted that they keep information about us?

What if the government printed all the documentation they have about us?

It would use billions of tons of paper, and a million rain forests would suffer.

What if the government deleted all the information they keep about us?

What if we could spy on and bug the government and find out what's really going on?

What if governments are spying on and bugging each other?

They do, according to the whistle-blower Edward Snowden.

What if the Government read all your private e-mails?

Thevwwries, like the USA.

What if the Government monitors your use of Internet?

They do, at least in some countries, like the USA.

What if no government had any surveillance?

What if we could have fair trials?

What if you become an enemy of the government?

You might, if you are a whistle-blower.

What if the government appreciated whistle-blowers instead of trying to take them down and accusing them of being traitors?

What if you were abused by the tax authorities?

It happens—all the time!

What if you consider criticizing the tax authority?

Don't even think about it. They will take revenge!

What if you were abused by your parents?

It happens—all the time!

What if we could stop all child abuse in the world?

What if you were abused by your own government?

It happens—all the time!

What if you were innocent but had to go to jail?

It happens—all the time!

What if you were abused by your partner or spouse?

It happens—all the time!

What if you were abused by your employer?

It happens—all the time!

What if you were abused by your children?

It happens—all the time!

What if the government is threatening you?

It happens—too often!

What if we could stop all this abuse?

What if you could save the life of a child abuser?

Would you save him or her, or would you just close your eyes?

What if you could save the life of a rapist?

Would you save him or her, or would you just close your eyes?

What if rapists and child abusers were castrated without anesthetic and jailed for life for their crime?

They would probably not do it again.

What if Saddam Hussein had not been arrested and executed?

In 2004, Saddam Hussein (1937-2006) was found guilty of the murder, torture, and illegal arrest of many people. His arrest was probably a big step towards democracy in Iraq.

What if the world's worst dictators had never lived?

The worst dictators have caused the deaths of millions of people.

Dictators responsible for more than twenty million deaths: Adolf Hitler (1889-1945, Germany), Joseph Stalin (1878-1953, USSR), and Mao Tse-Tung (1893-1976, China).

Dictators responsible for at least one million deaths: King Leopold II (1835-1909, Belgium), Kaiser Wilhelm II (1859-1941, Germany), Czar Nicholas II (1868-1918, Russia), Military Enver Pasha (1881-1922, Turkey), Vladimir Lenin (1870-1924, USSR), Emperor Hirohito (1901-1989, Japan), Prime Minister Hirota Koki (1878-1948, Japan), Prime Minister Jojo Hideki (1884-1948, Japan), President Chiang Kai-shek (1887-1975, China/Taiwan), President Ho Chi Minh (1890-1969, North Vietnam), President Kim II Sung (1912-1994, North Korea), President Yahya Khan (1917-1980, Pakistan), President Saddam

Hussein (1937-2006, Iraq), Prime Minister Pol Pot (1925-1998, Cambodia) and President Kim Jong Il (1942-2011, North Korea).[1]

What if these dictators had all lived at the same time?

What if there was no racism?

---

[1]   Wikipedia

Alcohol

What if whisky and cognac had not been invented?

The distillation of alcohol probably began in Babylon (now Iraq) in the second millennium BC. Legend has it that whisky has been produced in Scotland since the fifth century, but the earliest record states that it was first distilled in 1494. It is difficult to state when cognac first appeared on the scene, but it was probably around the sixteenth century.

Tequila Ley .925, an international company, is associated with the prestigious Maison Dudognon Cognac Grande Champagne. Presented in an exquisite bottle as the finest, most expensive cognac in the world, Henri IV Dudognon Heritage is an exclusive elixir. It has been produced since 1776, aged in barrels for more than 100 years. The one and only cognac bottle in the world valued at $3.4 million, it is 4 kg of pure platinum, yellow gold, and 6,500 diamonds, containing100 centiliters of 100-year-old cognac.[2]

What if you could afford to buy the most expensive cognac?

Would you drink it?

---

[2]   The DNA of cognac: (12 Jan. 1013 last accessed.) http://www.most-expensive-cognac.com/dna.php

What if nobody drank alcohol?

How many fields or square kilometres are used for grapes, potatoes, or corn in the production of alcohol? If everyone stopped drinking alcohol and these fields were used for cultivating food crops instead, there would be more than enough food for everyone in the world. Is it fair that a large part of the world's population does not have enough food because someone wants a drink or two?

What if we just halved our alcohol consumption?

That would probably result in there being enough food for everyone.

What if we made a toast to the people who go without food day in and day out so that we can have our gin and tonic, tequila, cognac, wine, whisky, or beer?

What if you thought seriously about this the next time you want a drink?

What if we stopped being selfish and stopped drinking so much alcohol?

I am no better than anyone else—I bought two bottles of wine this morning. That might have given food on the table for a few persons.

What if people stopped judging each other?

Sorry, I did not meant to judge you if you enjoy alcohol.

What if there was no vodka in Russia?

The Russians might be sober then—after a few months, when the alcohol finally left their blood!

Cash

What if there were no ATMs around?

Would you spend less money without them? The first ATM, also called a 'hole in the wall', was invented by John Shepherd-Barron (1925-2010) and introduced in June 1967 at Barclays Bank in UK.

What if there were no cash around?

In a few years, that might be the situation if everyone keeps using credit cards.

Children

What if children did not have to work?

In December 2011, *Sacom, Chinese Advocacy for Workers' Rights*, published a report in which they exposed working conditions in Shenzhen and Dongguan.[3] The organization discovered children working in a factory with very poor conditions. Children are burned, separated from their families, and penalized if they use the toilet without permission. They have to eat insect-infested food and live among rats. These factories make products for Disney, LEGO, and Marks & Spencer. Do you want to buy presents for your children from these corporations next Christmas?

What if Walt Disney had not invented cartoons?

The film producer, director, screenwriter, voice actor, animator, entrepreneur, entertainer, international icon, and philanthropist, Walter Elias Disney (1901-1966), was an innovator in animation. Walt Disney received more awards and nominations than any other individual in history. He is most famous for Mickey Mouse and *Snow White and the Seven Dwarves*.

What if children were not allowed to play games like Angry Birds or Minecraft?

What if children were not allowed to use Xbox 360?

---

[3] Sacom. Looking for Mickey Mouse's Conscience Campain. 11 Dec 2007. (12 Aug. 1013 last accessed.) http://www.evb.ch/cm_data/SACOM_Disney_ report_11_12_07.pdf.

What if there were no sweets?

Would we survive?

What if we go biking without a helmet?

What if you could decide how much pocket money you should have?

How much do you think your parents should pay you? Why?

Christmas

What if nobody believed in Father Christmas?

What if you met him?

What if people did not celebrate Christmas?

Countries

What if Denmark had a national symbol?

Denmark's only national symbol is Tuborg beer (which tastes awful anyway).

What if Sweden had a better national symbol than Absolut vodka?

It tastes as bad as Tuborg!

What if Paris took down the old, rusty and ugly steel monument in the centre of the city called the Eiffel Tower?

Crime

What if there were no crimes in the world?

What if fingerprints had not been discovered?

The first modern fingerprint identification was completed in 1823 by Professor Johann Evangelist Purkinje (1787-1869); several others have since contributed to its development. Fingerprint identification is an important tool in combating crime.

What if somebody stole your identity?

What if you could insure your identity for theft?

You can.

Culture

What if the French were not so bloody arrogant?

It would be much nicer to travel to Paris if the inhabitants were less arrogant! Have you ever heard a French person speaking English? Paris is a beautiful city, but I don't go there because of these arrogant people. Visiting Paris by night, when most of its arrogant inhabitants are asleep, is an option worth considering if you really have to go there.

What if we never had artists like Rafael, Leonardo da Vinci, Michelangelo, Vincent van Gogh, and Picasso?

What if we did not have any table manners?

The French probably introduced table manners around the sixteenth century. If so, why don't they have table manners today?

What if you want to tell your friends about this book?

E-mail them, chat on Twitter and Facebook, tell them face to face, give it to them as a gift, call them, and surprise them.

What if Scotsmen did not wear kilts?

Why on earth do all Scotsmen wear skirts? Is it because they want their willies to hang loose?

What if the Scots were not so mean?

What else are the Scots famous for?

What if you had written a bestselling book?

Only six books have sold more than 100 million copies:

Charles Dickens, *A Tale of Two Cities*: 200 million

J.R.R. Tolkien, *The Lord of the Rings*: 150 million

Antoine de Saint-Exupèry, *The Little Prince* (*Le Petit Prince*): 140 million

J.R.R. Tolkien, *The Hobbit*: 100 million

Cao Xuegin, *Dream of the Red Chamber*: 100 million

Agatha Christie, *And Then There Were None*: 100 million

Other books like *The Bible, The Qur'an, The Communist Manifesto,* and *Quotations from Chairman Mao* are often reported as the most-printed and most-distributed books in the world, with hundreds of millions of copies believed to be in existence of each of them, but no exact figures exists.

What if you were asked to list the five most watched films?

Could you list them? No. 1, *Avatar*, No. 2, *Titanic*, No. 3, *Gone with the Wind*, No. 4 *ET: The Extra-Terrestrial,* and No. 5, *Star Wars*.

What if you were asked to list the five most popular songs of all time?

Could you list them? No. 1, *Thriller* by Michael Jackson; No. 2, *White Christmas*, Bing Crosby; No. 3, *Bohemian Rhapsody*, Queen; No. 4, *Stairway to Heaven*, Led Zeppelin; and No. 5, *You Raise Me Up*, Josh Groban.

Corruption

What if the Fédération Internationale de Football Association (FIFA) had admitted bribery and corruption and started to clean itself up instead of denying it?

In 2006, British reporter Andrew Jennings published *Foul! The Secret World of FIFA: Bribes, Vote-Rigging and Ticket Scandals.* The book detailed an alleged international cash-for-contracts scandal following the collapse of ISL, FIFA's marketing partner. Further, it also revealed how some football officials had been urged to repay the sweeteners they secretly received. The book also alleged that vote-rigging had occurred in the fight for Sepp Blatter's continued control of FIFA. The book, followed by the television program *Panorama*, was really painful for FIFA and their members. The truth hurts when it is laid out on the table.

What if FIFA members had not been pissed off by Andrew Jennings and the BBC program *Panorama*?

Would FIFA then have given the World Cup to England in 2018 or 2022? England was probably the best candidate for the World Cup, but that did not help, as BBC published the very unpleasant truth about FIFA just a few days before FIFA members voted for the World Cup host countries.

What if former FIFA president and IOC member Joao Havelange had not resigned days before a critical hearing was to take place?

Joao Havelange was a member of the International Olympic Committee for forty-eight years and president of FIFA from 1974 to 1998. BBC's *Panorama* claimed in 2010 that Havelange had accepted money from ISL for granting lucrative World Cup contracts. Was it just a coincidence that he resigned just a few days before the hearing? Or was he afraid that more truth would come to the surface? Anyway, his resignation was extremely good timing, as he avoided the hearing.

Dark History

What if Great Britain didn't have a dark history?

During the first and second Opium Wars (1839-1842 and 1856-1860) between Great Britain and China, China was forced to open its borders to opium. The Opium Wars were the start of China's 'century of humiliation'; probably millions of Asians became addicted to opium. For Great Britain, the enormous profit was more important.

Shame on you, Great Britain!

What if Germany didn't have a dark history?

There is no need to speak of anything more than Hitler and his associates.

Shame on you, Germany!

What if Norway and Sweden didn't have a dark history?

In the book *Fatal Misconception: The Struggle to Control World Population,* Matthew Connelly describes how Norway and Sweden contributed to significant sterilization programs in India. Connelly told the true story of how family planners from developed countries forced through a reduction in the population among the world's poorest and how the wealthier countries deceived developing countries. Norway has a central place in this history, as the Norwegian Agency for Development Cooperation (NORAD) financed the sterilization of five million Indian women. Norway's dark history went on until 1995.

Shame on you, Norway!

What if the United States didn't have a dark history?[4]

One of the very dark sides of US history is how they treated Native Americans:

> *They were scalped; their brains knocked out; the men used their knives, ripped open women, clubbed little children, knocked them in the head with their guns, beat their brains out, mutilated their bodies in every sense of the world.*[5]

The United States took the basic of existence from them and forced them to move around because they wanted the land where the Indians had lived for generations.

Shame on you, United States!

What if China didn't have a dark history?

In June 1989, the Tiananmen Square protests took place: student-led popular demonstrations in Beijing. The protests were forcibly suppressed by hard-line leaders who ordered the military to enforce martial law in the country's capital. The crackdown resulted in troops with assault rifles and tanks attacking thousands of unarmed

---

[4]   Gaulin Grete. "Norges Mørke Historie" (Norways Dark History). *Ny Tid,* 8 May 2008.

[5]   U.S. Cong., Senate, 39 Cong., 2nd Sess., "The Chivington Massacre," Reports of the Committees.

civilians in Tiananmen Square, which student demonstrators had occupied for seven days.

Shame on you, China!

What if Russia didn't have a dark history?

No need to say more than Stalin and Lenin.

Shame on you, Russia!

What if France didn't have a dark history?

In 1954, Algeria was under French rule, and the people demanded independence, but France refused to give up the colony. Arbitrary arrests, torture, and executions suppressed the rebellion. The paratroop command group had no scruples, and their behavior put a strain on France's international reputation.

By the way, French soldiers had the right to have sex with prostitutes once a month and they used tanks to visit brothels. The French taxpayers were probably not very happy with the way the commando soldiers spent their money.[6]

Another dark history of France is Drancy, which was a World War II transit camp where around 70,000 French Jews were rounded up by their own countrymen, stuffed into railroad boxcars, and shipped off to Nazi concentration camps. It was the Frenchmen and not the Germans who did this.

Shame on you, France!

---

[6]   Illustrert Vitenskap Historie, June 2012.

What if South Africa didn't have a dark history?

No need to say more than human rights, apartheid, and racism.

Shame on you, South Africa!

What if the churches had no dark history?

Child abuse is not acceptable, not even in the name of the religion. Further, it is not acceptable to ignore it, which priests have done for centuries.

Shame on you, all priests around the world who have abused children. Also, shame on all priests who closed their eyes to these horrible abuses.

There is no forgiveness for such abuse.

What if you have any example of dark histories?

Submit them on our web page: *www.whatif.uk.com.*

What if Spain had to pay back to the colony countries what they stole from them during the colony period?

During the colony period (1500-1650), Spain took about 180 tons of gold and 16,000 tons of silver from USA back to Spain. The also took all other recourses they could find like, slaves and all other natural resources they could find. The value of only the gold and silver today would be

180,000 kg gold   USD 6.923.571.429
16000000 kg silver   USD 9.948.051.948
5 % interest from year 1575

During the period 1500-1650 Spain confiscated around 180 tons of Gold and 16,000 tons of Silver from USA and brought it back to Spain[7]. The value today would have been USD . . . for the Gold and USD . . . for the silver. The value of the late interest fee from 1575 until today would have been USD . . . Spain probably also confiscated a lot of other resources from the USA inclusive slaves.

Spain would have been bankruptcy and USA would have a far better economic situation than they actually got today if Spain would have to repay what they stole.

How much did Spain, England, the Netherlands and Portugal confiscate from all the colonies?

---

[7]   All Verdens History, *Discovery of America 1492,* page 18,(5/2013)

Death

What if you woke up one morning and noticed that you were dead?

If you woke up, you cannot be dead, and if you are dead, you do not wake up!

What if you died without writing your last will and testament?

It would definitely not be your problem, but what about your children? Would they start to fight, become enemies, take the case to the court, or perhaps never talk to each other again? There is often disagreement between those who hope to benefit from an inheritance, even when it is a modest amount. A will might save your children a lot of trouble.

What if you followed John Grisham's example?

In his book, *The Last Will*, the beneficiaries were disinherited if they argued over the testator's will.

What if you had a bucket list of things you wanted to do before you die?

What would be on your list?

What if you knew what happens after death?

What if you could postpone your death?

For how long?

What if you could save a life by risking your own life?

Development

What if there were no oil or gas left?

What if iron did not exist?

What if Einstein had not developed his theory of relativity (the geometric theory of gravitation, E = mc²)?

Theoretical physicist Albert Einstein (1879-1955) developed his theory in 1916 and was considered a genius. However, three Nobel Prize winners in physics, Saul Perlmutter, Adam Riess, and Brian Schmidt, later questioned whether Einstein's theory is correct.

What if the atom had never been discovered?

The Greek philosopher Democritus (460-370 BC) was the first to discover the particle of life and called it an atom (indivisible). The existence of the atom is one of the most fundamental and pervasive elements of scientific knowledge that we have. The discovery of the atom was further developed by philosopher, chemist, and physicist Robert Boyle (1627-1691) and chemist, meteorologist, and physicist John Dalton (1766-1844).[8]

What if stamps had not been introduced?

---

[8]   Wikipedia

What if we did not have the mètre?

Back in the 1700s, there were 250,000 different ways to measure distance in France. In 1791, the *Acadèmie des Sciences* decided to introduce one measurement system. It took several years to measure the correct metre, and it was decided that the metre should be one ten-millionth part of the distance from the North Pole to the equator. The reason that the metre was introduced was to establish a simpler and fairer tax system and in order to avoid misunderstanding in the military.[9]

What if there were no color at all?

Can you imagine a world without color: only black, white, and grey? For thousands of years, red cloth was very valuable because red dye was so rare, and kings forbade people from using the color. Around 1500, the Spanish found the perfect red dye. Both pirates and spies tried to steal the formula, and rulers spent a fortune to get hold of it.

What if we did not have the flush toilet?

In 2011, 40 per cent of the world's population still has no access to a toilet of any kind. The flush toilet was invented in 1596. When Louis XIV of France, the Sun King (1638-1715), held court, he often did so from his toilet surrounded by courtiers. Did you know there is a group called the World Toilet Organization?

What if plastics had not been invented?

In 1862, metallurgist and inventor Alexander Parkes (1813-1890) invented plastic. In 2011, the UK used nearly 300,000 tonnes

---

[9]   Illustrert Vitenskap 2013

of plastic bottles. It is believed that about 100,000 animals are killed each year from ingesting or becoming entangled in plastic. Most plastics are non-biodegradable, which means they will take hundreds or perhaps thousands of years to decompose.

What if people were not adaptable?

What if we had not been able to build skyscrapers?

In 1855, the first modern skyscraper was built in Chicago; the city's inhabitants were extremely impressed, having never seen anything like it. The building had ten floors and was an unbelievable forty-two metres high. In 2010, Dubai built an 830-metre skyscraper, Burj Khalifa, and there are plans to build a skyscraper one kilometre high. Would you live on the top floor of a building one kilometre high? You would almost be able to knock on God's front door!

What if we could teach everyone to read?

The United Nations Educational, Scientific and Cultural Organization (UNESCO) estimates that around 860 million people (around 17 per cent of the world's population) are illiterate.

What if we did not have tinned products?

What if we did not have porcelain?

Posh people would starve! Eating on something other than porcelain? That would be disgusting!

What if Martin Luther King had not fought for civil rights in the United States?

Economics

What if you owned a 1908 Model-T Ford?

What would it be worth today? The amount someone would be willing to pay, not a penny more, but probably more than the $290 it cost new.

What if Greece, Spain, Portugal, Ireland, or the United States went bankrupt?

Here are a few things that would happen if these countries went bankrupt:[10]

Every bank in Greece would instantly become insolvent.

The Greek government would nationalise every bank in the country.

The Greek government would forbid withdrawals from Greek banks.

To prevent Greek depositors from rioting in the streets, the Greek government would declare a curfew, perhaps even martial law.

Greece would re-denominate all its debts into 'New Drachmas' (or whatever the new currency would be called). This is a classic ploy of defaulting countries.

---

[10]   Lilico Andrew. "What happens when Greece defaults?" *The Telegraph,* 20 May 2011.

The New Drachma would devalue by some 30-70 per cent (probably around 50 per cent), effectively defaulting on 50 per cent or more of all Greek euro-denominated debts.

The Irish would, within a few days, walk away from the debts of its banking system.

The Portuguese government would wait to see whether there is chaos in Greece before deciding whether to default in turn.

A number of French and German banks would make enough loss to no longer meet regulatory capital adequacy requirements.

The European Central Bank (ECB) would become insolvent, given its very high exposure to Greek government debt and the Greek and Irish banking sectors' debts.

The French and German governments would meet to decide whether (a) to recapitalise the ECB, or (b) to allow the ECB to print money to restore its solvency. Because the ECB has relatively little foreign currency-denominated exposure, it could in principle print its way out of trouble, but this is forbidden under its founding charter. On the other hand, the EU treaty explicitly forbids the form of bailouts used for Greece, Portugal, and Ireland, but a little thing like being blatantly illegal hasn't prevented it from happening, so its illegality will not prove much of a hurdle.

They would recapitalise their own banks, but declare an end to all bailouts.

There would be carnage in the market for Spanish banking sector bonds, as bondholders anticipate imposed debt-equity swaps.

This assumption would prove justified as the Spaniards choose to over-ride the structure of current bond contracts in the Spanish banking sector, recapitalizing a number of banks via debt-equity swaps.

Bondholders would take the Spanish banking sector to the European Court of Human Rights, and in all likelihood other courts as well, claiming violations of property rights. These cases won't be heard for years. By the time they are finally heard, no one will care.

Attention would turn to the British banks (and others).

In one word: Chaos!

What if all these countries went bankrupt at the same time?

Would it be a worldwide financial crisis like we have never seen before?

What if you need insurance?

Hurry up and get one.

What if the Wall Street crash of 1929 had never happened?

The stock market crash was the most devastating financial crisis in the history of the United States, and it lasted for twelve years. Thousands of businesses closed; unemployment increased significantly; lots of rich people and business were bankrupted; and many suffered lifelong debt. The main reason for the crash was that people were greedy, believing they could make a fortune playing the stock market and thinking it was impossible to lose money on shares.

What if it happened again?

It will.

What if all share prices in the world suddenly fell by 25 per cent?

Would you buy or sell?

What if share prices worldwide suddenly increased by25 per cent?

Would you buy or sell?

What if your house burned down and you were not insured?

What if nobody could make money on shares?

What if nobody could lose money on shares?

What if you got an overdraft of £1 for ten days?

The bank could charge you £6 per day. That's robbery!

What if there were no banks?

What if no one had established the accounting system?

Accountancy is the process of communicating financial information about a business to stakeholders, such as shareholders, investors, managers, and the government. Accounting is thousands of years old. The earliest accounting records, dating back more than 7,000 years, were found in Mesopotamia (Assyria). Today, accountancy is based on the double-entry bookkeeping principle, which first emerged in northern Italy in the fourteenth century.

What if there were no business people?

What if you were super rich?

What if patents had not been introduced?

A patent protects your ideas and gives you the right to exclude others from selling, using, or making your invention without paying you for the right to do so.

What if nobody had thought of the safety pin?

Mechanic Walter Hunt (1796-1859) took out a patent on the safety pin in 1849.

What if capitalism had never been developed?

What if cheques had never been introduced?

The cheque originates from the ancient bank system, when the bill of exchange was used as a cheque.

What if bank transfers were impossible?

What if you could not register your immovable properties in the land registry?

The registration gives you protection so nobody else can claim ownership to your property.

What if you were really poor?

What if nobody invested in shares?

What if you got a larger mortgage than you could cope with?

What if your bank went bankrupt?

Banks can go bankrupt. Would your savings be safe?

What if you went bankrupt?

What if you had no insurance for your mortgage and you became disabled or died?

If you became disabled, you would have a problem. If you died, your spouse, partner, or children would have a problem.

What if you were involved in a car accident and your car was uninsured?

What if you spend more money than you earn?

If you do not have any savings, you might get into trouble quite quickly.

What if you had to pay 23,707 per cent interest on your credit card when you take out cash?

In fact, this might be what you are charged if you take out cash on your credit card. If you had low credit, A Swedish company would charge you 23,703 per cent! Don't use your credit card as a cash machine.

What if China becomes the world's leading economy?

They might.

What if nobody cheated insurance companies?

Could premiums be reduced for the rest of us? Are honest people paying for people who cheat?

What if people weren't so greedy?

Greedy investors often put their financial situation at risk because they thought they were invincible and it was impossible to lose their investment.

The first modern finance crisis was the Dutch Tulip Mania in 1637. The tulip bulb was the ultimate object for investment, and investors thought the price would go skyward, which it did, but most people thought it would increase even further. In 1637, one single bulb had an unbelievable value of USD 893,000 (2011 value); investors thought they made a good investment when they paid this for one single bulb. It was impossible to lose on this investment, until the bubble burst. When the hysteria was at its worst, one single tulip bulb cost 2,500 Dutch guilders; for the same amount, investors could have bought all of the following:[11]

> 5,200 kg of wheat: 448 guilders
> 10,400 kg of rye: 558 guilders
> Four big ox: 480 guilders
> Eight big pigs: 240 guilders
> Twelve sheep: 120 guilders
> Two large barrels of wine: 70 guilders

---

[11] Illustrert Vitenskap Historie, Jan 2006.

Four barrels of beer: 32 guilders
Two tons of butter: 192 guilders
100 pounds (450 kg) of cheese: 120 guilders
A bed with linen: 100 guilders
A dress: 80 guilders
A drinking vessel of silver: 60 guilders

Total: 2,500 guilders

And the greedy investors thought the price would increase further. Unbelievable!

Then there was the Mississippi bubble in 1719-1720, when France National Bank issued shares in the newly established Mississippi Company; shareholders were promised a gain of 120 per cent. The bubble burst when investors discovered that the company was not worth the value of its shares.

The next bubble that burst was the South Sea bubble in 1720, when the South Sea Company promised to pay off the British government's debt. The company collapsed a few months later, with a 75 per cent decrease in the share price.

From 1996 to 2000, investors put billions into dotcom companies, which hadn't even made a penny at that time. A crash was unavoidable, but the investors didn't see it coming until it was too late.

What if greedy investors learned from previous mistakes?

What if you had a million dollar to invest; what would you invest in?

What if you could not open a bank account?

What if all countries had the same currency?

What if you had no mortgage at all?

What if you could receive a penny every time someone had a fag?

You would be rich (very rich).

What if you could find a new business niche?

Remember, many successful businesses started in the kitchen or garage.

What if you could have a bank loan when you really needed it?

Bank loans are like someone lending you an umbrella on a sunny day and asking you to give it back when it rains.

What if you are a millionaire with no heirs?

The government will benefit from the inheritance.

What if you owned E-bay?

What if Adam Smith had not written *Wealth of Nations*?

Adam Smith's (1723-1790) *Wealth of Nations* was a fundamental work on classical economics; written in 1776, the book is still valid today.

What if there was no shadow economy?

According to Friedrich Schneider, an economics professor at Johannes Kepler Universität in Austria, the Italian shadow economy accounts for 21.2 per cent of the country's GNP, which is 300 billion Euros.[12]

What if the value of the bitcoins had a crack like the tulip crack?

It might very well be a crack.

---

[12]   Schneider Friedrich, Svart økonomi har holdt Italia flytende (Shadow economy has kept Italy alive) *E24.no*, 9 Nov. 2011.

Education

What if there were no schools or universities?

What if you could do whatever education you wanted?

What if your university was not accredited?

Family

What if you survived an abortion?

What if your loved one(s) suddenly left you?

What if your children did not want to speak to you?

What if your parents did not want to speak to you?

What if your partner or spouse wanted to go in one direction and you wanted to go in another one?

What if your child needed a kidney transplant and you were the only who matched?

What if your brother or sister needed a kidney transplant?

What if a family member you did not know about turned up?

What if your closest relative was declared brain dead and you had to decide whether to donate their organs?

What if nobody could divorce?

What if your parents disinherited you?

You would not inherit their debt either, so it might be beneficial if they disinherited you.

What if there were no care homes for the elderly?

What if you did not have any family?

What if you had to marry someone you did not love or perhaps not even knew?

Even in 2013, there are many arranged marriages; people still have to marry someone they do not know or love.

What if your only son told you he was gay?

What if your only daughter told you she was lesbian?

What if your parents did not have a pension or savings when they retired?

Would that be their problem or yours?

What if your boyfriend or girlfriend proposed to you?

Yes or no?

What if you proposed to your boyfriend or girlfriend and he or she said no?

What if you drove with your child in your car?

Would they be safe?

What if your husband, wife, partner, girlfriend, or boyfriend were not so irritating?

What if your parents were not so irritating?

What if your children were not so irritating?

What if you were not so irritating?

What if your husband, wife, partner, girlfriend, or boyfriend could be quiet for ten minutes?

What if your son or daughter was jailed?

What if you found out that your son-in-law is beating your daughter?

Fear

What if you were about to talk to a thousand people and got stage fright?

What if a murder moved in next door in your neighborhood?

What if a rapist moved in next door in your neighborhood?

Fiction

What if nobody was curious or imaginative?

Would anything have been invented?

Would there have been any development?

Would we still be living in the Stone Age?

Would any diseases have been cured?

Would we be educated?

Would we be able to produce food?

Would anything be different?

What if we did not need to sleep?

What would you do with eight more hours every day?

What if you could change one thing you regret saying or doing?

What if you could find a horoscope that told you all the truth?

What if the week didn't have seven days?

Ancient Egyptian and Chinese civilizations had a ten-day week. If we had a ten-day week, would we have to work eight days a week, or would we have a five-day weekend?

What if the sun burned out?

What if it never rained?

What if all the ice in the Arctic and Antarctic melted?

There is so much ice in the world that if it all melted, sea levels would rise hugely across the world, perhaps as much as eighty metres. Say goodbye to London, New York, Sydney, Bangkok, and Rio—in fact, the majority of the world's major cities. Indigenous Arctic peoples would find their food stocks gone, while fresh water supplies in Asia and South America would disappear as the glaciers melt away. The habitats of penguins, polar bears, and seals would disappear, and the traditional lives of indigenous peoples would no longer be possible. However, according to principal investigator at the British Antarctic Survey, David Vaughan:

> It is not going to happen on any realistic human timescale; it's so cold that you could raise temperatures by 5 to 10°C without having much of an impact; it's on rock above sea level, so warming in the ocean can't affect it.[13]

What if the world were 2 to 4°C warmer?

---

[13]   Black Richard. "Earth—melting in the heath?" *BBC News Channel*. 18 May 2007. (12 Aug. 1013 last accessed.) http://news.bBC.co.uk/1/hi/sci/tech/4315968.stm.

What if the world were 2 to 4°C colder?

What if the dinosaurs had survived?

What if every person over 18 years old worked one hour more each day?

Would that boost the economy or would it mean more unemployed people?

What if everyone lived one year longer?

What if you killed somebody while driving under the influence of alcohol?

What if you could rule the world for one day?

What if everyone had the same tastes or interests?

What if you did not have any friends?

What if every person in the world had the same amount of money?

After a few months or even days, some of them would be much richer, some would be poorer, and some probably bankrupt.

What if you drove without car insurance and caused a serious accident?

Would you feel guilty and be in debt for life?

What if you won $100 million in the lottery?

What if we could look into the future?

What if the population on the earth was twenty billion?

What if every couple in the world had one more child?

What if you could travel back in time?

You can, if you fly from east to west and cross several time zones. You might arrive the day before you left.

What if you could travel into the future?

What if there were no trees?

What if there were no flowers?

What if there were no insects?

What if you could stop time?

What if there were no pollution?

What if the clock went backwards?

Would we get younger each hour?

What if you had unlimited power to do whatever you wanted for one day?

What if you could be your own grandparent for one day?

What if you could be your own parent for one day?

Would you increase your pocket money, stop nagging, never ask your children to go to bed or clean up their room?

What if you had several children and, in the event of a tragedy, you could only save one of them?

What if you had to save one of your parents?

What if you could be another person?

What if Muslims could eat pork?

What if we didn't have toothbrushes?

The toothbrush wasn't patented until 1941 (by Frank E Wolcott).

What if everyone spoke the same language?

What if there were no speed limits on the roads?

What if Pythagoras had not questioned the idea of a flat earth?

Greek philosopher Pythagoras (580-500 BC) was one of the first people to believe the earth was round (or at least the first who dared to admit it).

What if you could meet one famous person?

What if you could travel back in time and meet a historic person?

What if you could choose one location in the world to visit?

Where would it be?

What if there is life after death?

Since the beginnings of humankind, people have wondered whether there is life after death. Billions have died, but nobody knows. The Great Pyramid of Giza is the oldest human-made structure built for the afterlife. Hinduism and Buddhism teach that the soul is reborn after death.

What if we didn't have neighbours?

What if people in the UK had to drive on the right side of the road?

Seventy-six countries, including seven European countries, have left-hand traffic, which is 33.9 per cent of the world's population. Countries that still have left-hand traffic include the UK, Australia, New Zealand, India, Pakistan, Malaysia, South Africa, Thailand, and Japan. Sweden, for example, changed to right-hand drive in 1968, but back then there were only a few Volvos and Saabs on the roads.

What if you took a few polar bears to the South Pole, where there are penguins?

What if Paris didn't have the Eiffel Tower?

The Eiffel Tower (324 metres high) was built in 1889 as the entrance for the 1889 World's Fair. Structural engineer Gustave Eiffel (1832-1923) designed the tower, which was meant to be disassembled after the fair. It is the icon of Paris and one of the most recognizable and visited structures in the world.[14]

What if the Eiffel Tower had been disassembled after the World's Fair, as was planned?

So what?

What if New York didn't have the Statue of Liberty?

The Statue of Liberty (93 metres high) has become an icon of freedom and of the United States; it was dedicated in 1886. It was a gift from France, contributed by around 120,000 people. The statue was built in France and then transported to New York.[15]

What if Gustave Eiffel had mixed up the drawings of the Statue of Liberty and the Eiffel Tower and built the Statue of Liberty in Paris and the Eiffel Tower in New York?

What if you met your double?

You could send him or her to your job and have a day off.

What if you received a Nobel Prize by mistake?

What if something happened to you?

Are you insured? If not, have you thought about the consequences?

---

[14]   Wikipedia
[15]   Ibid

What if we could stop all bullying?

What a wonderful world that would be for pupils, students, colleagues, neighbours, partners, children, and parents.

What if you really wanted something?

Could you get it?

What if you could meet a legend?

Who would you meet and why?

What if the legend was dead?

Would you still meet them? How? And where? The legend would not return to life, so you would have to go wherever they were. Would you still want to meet them?

Food

What if we did not have knives and forks (or chopsticks)?

Knives have been used for millions of years. Bronze forks have been used since the eighth century. In Northern Europe, the church was skeptical about the fork, as there was nothing in the Bible stating that Jesus Christ had used one. Did he have bad table manners back then?

What if McDonald's were closed down?

McDonald's is the world's largest fast food restaurant. According to their 2010 annual report, they serve around sixty-four million customers daily in 119 countries. The company was founded by Richard and Maurice McDonald in 1948; they established the (unhealthy) fast-food concept. In 1954-55, they sold it to Ray Kroc (1902-1984). Kroc sold multi-mixer milkshake machines, and he bought McDonald's because he thought he would sell more machines if he owned McDonald's, and he probably did.

What if Richard and Maurice McDonald's surname had been McSmith instead?

What if there were no corn?

What if it started to snow in the desert?

What if Will Kellogg had not liked cereals?

Will and John Kellogg sold health food; in 1906, they invented cornflakes by accident after some corn was burnt. Cornflakes were not a success until sugar was added. In 2012, Kellogg earned USD14.2 billion and had 31,000 employees. Not bad considered that the company's success was based on an accident.

What if Nestlé had not introduced an alternative to breast milk?

It all started with an alternative to breast milk. In 1860, confectioner Henri Nestlé (1814-1890) gave a substitution for breast milk to a premature baby who could not tolerate its mother's milk; the child might have died without this alternative. The news spread, and he established the Nestlé Company in 1905. In 2010, Nestlé had 281,000 employees and was present in more than eighty countries, with a turnover of 109,722 million CHF.[16]

What if we could take a pill instead of food each day?

It would probably be boring to go to a restaurant, but on the other hand, you would not have to spend time shopping or washing dishes.

What if no one had to go to bed hungry?

A big part of the world's population does—every day!

---

[16] Nestlé, http://www.nestle.com/AboutUs/KeyFigures/Pages/KeyFigures.aspx.

What if the English could cook?

They think they can, but the only thing they can make is fish and chips. The fish is never fresh and chips are deep fried in oil that should have been thrown away months before.

What if no fields were used to produce cereal for brewing beer?

Today, the beer industry is worth billions of dollars; it requires farming a vast amount of land. What if these fields were used for producing food for the poor instead?

What if we had not eaten any sweets?

If the fields were used for production of food instead, there would probably be enough food for everyone in the world.

Football

What if your favorite football team went bankrupt?

What if Manchester United, Liverpool, Chelsea, Arsenal, and Manchester City merged into one club?

What if England never had football?

So what? Do they really have football? They haven't won the World Cup since the Middle Ages anyway (well, 1966).

What if you could have two tickets to the World Cup final?

Would you sell them on the black market? You could probably earn a fortune. How much would the tickets be worth? A lot.

What if you had these tickets but left them home on the day of the match?

What if you had to support the team you hate most for one year?

Friends

What if your best friend became your worst enemy?

It happens—often.

What if you were forced to be friends with your enemy?

What if Words with Friends had not been invented?

What a wasteful time! Playing crossword-puzzle games with people you do not know. Get a life.

What if you turned the world upside down in order to help your friend and he or she did not say thank you?

Government

What if nobody wanted to work for the government?

Well, many of them don't work anyway. It would be less bureaucracy, probably less taxes, fewer incompetent politicians, less overspending, and so on.

What if politicians started to be honest and stopped lying?

Health

What if you do not know how to give first aid and are the first one at the scene of an accident?

You might be able to save a life if you know first aid! Remember, the aims of first aid are:

- saving lives,
- prevent further harm, and
- start the recovery process.

What if you could recognize when somebody was having a stroke?

You can! Remember the first three letters: S. T. R. S: Ask the individual to Smile. T: Ask the person to Talk coherently. R: Ask them to Raise both arms. Another sign of a stroke is if you ask the person to stick out their tongue and it goes to one side or the other.

Neurologists say that if stroke victims receive treatment within three hours, the effects can be totally reversed. The trick is recognizing when a stroke is happening and then getting the patient medical attention.

Recognizing a stroke:

- Read and learn! Symptoms of a stroke can be difficult to identify. Unfortunately, a lack of awareness spells disaster. The stroke victim may suffer severe brain damage if no one recognizes the symptoms. Doctors now say bystanders can recognize a stroke by following the three simple steps listed above.

- If the person has trouble with any of these tasks, call the emergency number *immediately* and describe the symptoms to the dispatcher.

What if you could stop smoking?

You can—if you *really* want to.

What if you become seriously ill or disabled?

What if Alexander Fleming had not discovered penicillin?

Biologist and pharmacologist Alexander Fleming (1881-1955) discovered the enzyme lysozyme in 1923 and penicillin in 1928; he shared the Nobel Prize in 1945 with Howard Florey (1898-1968) and Ernst Boris Chain (1906-1979).[17]

What if you became blind?

What if you became deaf?

What if you need information regarding health care, including a symptom checklist or pharmacy information?

You could log into WebMD, but I would prefer to call my doctor.

What if you had no sense of taste?

What if you could not remember?

---

[17]   Wikipedia

What if public health care didn't exist?

What if everyone stopped eating unhealthy food?

What if there were no hospitals?

What if you had no tongue?

What if there were no medicines?

What if there were no anesthetic?

What if you had no legs or toes?

What if we could not give blood?

What if no disease could be cured?

What if all disease could be cured?

What if we could not put a broken arm or leg in a cast?

What if you only ate unhealthy food?

What if you did not exercise?

What if organ transplantations were not possible?

The heart, kidneys, eyes, liver, lungs, pancreas, intestine, and thymus can all be transplanted.

What if you became an organ donor?

You might save a life.

What if you had to lose one sense: would you choose blindness, being speechless, or deafness?

What if you lost all your teeth?

What if you lost all your hair?

What if you could not take a shower for ninety days?

What if there was no pain relief?

What if your children started to smoke?

It happens—too often. Even though smoking is responsible for the death of thousands of people every day, people continue smoking.

What if you could lose weight?

You can—if you *really* want to.

What if you could not have your daily cup(s) of tea or coffee?

I am not sure I could survive without my fifteen cups of coffee—every morning. Could you?

What if you lost your mind?

What if you had no skin?

What if . . . you had a drink problem?

There is help and support available, but *you* need to take the first step.

What if you have a gambling problem?

There is help and support available, but *you* need to take the first step.

What if you have a drug problem?

There is help and support available, but *you* need to take the first step.

What if somebody found a cure for cancer?

What if we could not measure the temperature of sick people?

What if Hippocrates had not introduced the current approach to medicine 2,500 years ago?

Hippocrates (460 B.C.-377 B.C.) came up with this highly relevant advice:

> *First we must consider the nature of man in general and of each individual, and the characteristics of each disease. Then, we must consider the patient, what food is given to him and who gives it, for this may make it easier for him to take or more difficult, the conditions of climate and locality both in general and in particular, the patient's customs, mode of life, pursuits, and age. Then we must consider his speech, his mannerisms, his silences, his thoughts, his habits of sleep or wakefulness, and his dreams, their nature and time.*
>
> *Next, we must note whether he plucks his hair, scratches, or weeps. We must observe his*

paroxysms, his stools, urine, sputum, and vomit. We look for any change in the state of the malady; how often such changes occur, and their nature, and the particular change which induces death or a crisis. Observe, too, sweating, shivering, chill, cough, sneezing, hiccough, the kind of breathing, belching, wind, whether silent or noisy, hemorrhages, and hemorrhoids. We must determine the significance of all these signs.[18]

[18] Hippokrates. The famous people. (13 Aug. 1013 last accessed.) http://www. famoushistoricalevents.net/hippocratic-method/

History

What if the ten worst epidemics had never occurred?

How many people would there be on the earth today? These are ten worst diseases throughout history:[19]

-   Scarlet fever: this illness caused as many as 25 per cent of all deaths (the total number of deaths is uncertain) at the end of the nineteenth century.
-   Measles: estimated deaths from measles during World War I was three million.
-   Typhoid fever: same number of deaths during World War I as measles.
-   Cholera: estimated deaths of more than forty million, mainly during the nineteenth century.
-   AIDS: estimated deaths of twenty-five million since the 1980s, with forty million currently living with the HIV infection.
-   Black death: estimated deaths of around 100 million, mainly in the early fourteenth century.
-   Tuberculosis: estimated 100 million fatalities, with around 1.5 million new victims every year.
-   Spanish flu: between 50 million and 100 million deaths, mainly during 1918-1919.
-   Smallpox: estimated deaths of 500 million, up to the beginning of the twentieth century. The world is now declared smallpox free.

---

[19] Wikipedia

- Malaria: estimated deaths of 300 million during the last 100 years.

What if Christopher Columbus had not completed his voyages across the Atlantic Ocean, which led to Europe's awareness of the American continent?

Explorer, colonizer, and navigator Christopher Columbus (1451-1506) completed four voyages across the Atlantic Ocean. Some of his crew was murderers or bandits who had been put in prison for life. They were given the choice of staying in prison or joining Columbus on his voyages, without knowing whether they would return. At this time, many people thought the earth was flat and it was possible to sail off the edge. Even so, many of the criminals took the risk and joined him.

What if people had not learned how to control fire?

It is believed that human beings were able to make use of fire 400,000 years ago, though evidence of cooked food is found from1.9 million years ago.

What if there had been no Industrial Revolution in the UK in the eighteenth century?

The Industrial Revolution brought about major changes in manufacturing, agriculture, mining, transportation, and technology, significantly improving living standards. It was perhaps the most important economic event in modern times. Employees thought they would lose their jobs and protested, destroying the new machinery to stop the development.

What if Cambridge University had not formed the Football Association and invented the modern game of soccer in 1863?

Football is probably the most popular sport in the world.

What if China had not introduced the 'one child' policy in 1978?

Today, China's population is around 1.34 billion people. How big would the Chinese population be today without this policy?

What if Chinese families have more than one child?

They have to pay a large fine.

What if they could not afford to pay the fine?

What if we were still in the Stone Age?

What if nobody was interested in history?

What if the first engine-powered airplane had not been built?

The first engine-powered plane was designed and constructed by Orville Wright (1871-1948) and his brother, Wilbur (1867-1912), bicycle retailers and manufacturers; the first flight was in 1903.

What if Gillette had not invented the razor?

Inventor King Camp Gillette (1855-1932) introduced the modern razor in 1893; he sold 168 razors in 1903.

What if nobody was interested in archaeology?

Would we know anything about the past?

What if the September 11 attacks had never happened?

On 9/11/2001, there were four coordinated suicide attacks on the United States. 2,977 innocent people died. Let's never forget the victims. After 9/11, the security on flights was significantly improved. The world will never be the same again.

What if women had not been given the right to vote?

Women haven't always had the right to vote. Women in the UK started a riot in 1832 to fight for their rights, but they were not listened to until 1928. In 1893, New Zealand became the first country to give women the right to vote, followed by Finland in 1906, Norway in 1913, the United States in 1920, Switzerland in 1971, and Kuwait in 2007.

What if the Panama Canal had never been built?

The Panama Canal was opened in 1914 after chaos and tragedy, with more than 27,000 workers dying during its construction; 13,000 ships use the canal each year, which is far more efficient than sailing down the coast of South America to Cape Horn. More than one million ships have used the canal since it opened. In 1928, the author Richard Halliburton was the first man to swim the canal, after paying a thirty-six-cent weight fee.

What if London had not built the underground tube system?

The world's first railway under the ground was opened in London in 1863. The project was so comprehensive that no other city dared to do the same until forty years later. During World War II, the underground system was used as a massive air-raid shelter, saving many lives.

What if the heavy water sabotage in Norway had not succeeded?

The heroes from Telemark in Norway sabotaged a heavy water facility after the Allied Forces High Command in London determined that the Germans were developing an atomic reactor and nuclear bomb. Twelve men were handpicked to sabotage the factory. They destroyed the facility and large quantities of heavy water; it is considered to be one of the most heroic sabotage acts of World War II.[20]

What if Hitler had been able to use the heavy water?

Would World War II have ended differently?

What if the gramophone had not been invented?

In 1877, Thomas Alva Edison (1847-1931) demonstrated the first phonograph, or more exactly, he improved Leon Scott's phonautograph, while Emile Berliner (1851-1929) took this invention a step further and developed the gramophone, which he patented in 1901.

What if Victor Hugo had not written *The Hunchback of Notre Dame*?

Notre Dame in Paris is one of the world's most beautiful cathedrals, but around 1800, it was in such bad condition that serious consideration was given to demolishing it. In 1831, Victor Hugo wrote *The Hunchback of Notre Dame*, criticizing the government for its lack of maintenance; large numbers of people started to visit the cathedral, and it was saved. The contribution of Hugo, a poet,

---

[20] Norsk Hydro. '1943: The Heroes from Telemark.' Norsk Hydro. (12Aug. 2013 last Accessed.) http://www.hydro.com/en/About-Hydro/Our-history/1929-1945/1943-The-Heroes-of-Telemark/.

playwright, novelist, essayist, visual artist, statesman, and human rights activist, to saving the cathedral is impossible to evaluate. The cathedral was started in 1163 and completed in the 1240s.

What if Scotland had not become bankrupt in 1706?

From the Middle Ages, England had wanted to establish a union with Wales, Ireland, and Scotland, but Scotland was not interested in a union with England whatsoever. However, the combination of a financial crisis in Scotland, bribery by the English government, secret agents, and dirty behavior resulted in Scotland entering a union with England in 1706. Since then, the Scots have fought for independence from the rest of the union. In 2011, the Scottish National Party won an overall majority in parliament and intends to hold a referendum on independence from the UK.

What if Gandhi had preferred a legal career?

Mohandas K. Gandhi was educated as a lawyer, but his priority became the fight for an independent India. Great Britain had power over India since the colony period and was not interested in giving it independence. However, Gandhi fought for independence, succeeding in 1947, when Great Britain finally ended its colonial power over India and Pakistan.

What if the stock exchange had not been established?

The first stock market was the Amsterdam Stock Exchange, established in 1602.

What if the Jews had never been persecuted?

What if Napoleon had not invaded Russia in 1812 and lost 500,000 soldiers?

Would the outcome of the Battle of Waterloo in 1812 have been different if Napoleon had not lost these soldiers? He was defeated by Admiral Nelson.

What if we knew the secret of the pyramids?

What if the Roman Empire had never been established?

The establishment of the Roman Empire was the foundation of modern European civilization. The Roman influence goes deep into our laws and language; many of our institutions spring from the Roman models, and it is difficult to imagine what our lives would be like without it.

What if the Roman Empire had not been destroyed but had increased instead?

Would we now have the Roman Union instead of the European Union (EU)?

What if Napoleon's doctor had not introduced the ambulance?

In 1870, Napoleon's chief doctor introduced the forerunner of the modern ambulance service at the Battle of Spires.

What if the Cuban Missile Crisis had ended in a nuclear war?

It was very close—closer than most people realise.

What if Florence Nightingale had not been a nurse?

Florence Nightingale (1820-1910) founded professional nursing in 1860 with a school in London.

What if the Leaning Tower of Pisa leaned even more?

The Tower of Pisa was started in 1178, but the bell chamber was not finished until 1372. Before the restoration work in the 1990s, the tower leaned at an angle of 5.5 degrees, while it now leans at 3.99 degrees. It is believed that it started to lean because construction workers cut some corners. Typically Italian, to cut corners!

What if President Thomas Jefferson had not written the Declaration of Independence?

The declaration was written in 1776, the year America become independent. If President Jefferson (1743-1826) had not written it, would the United Sates still be part of British territories?

What if Amnesty International had never had been founded?

Amnesty International was founded in 1961; its objective is

> *to conduct research and generate action to prevent and end grave abuses of human rights, and to demand justice for those whose rights have been violated.*[21]

The group has more than three million members.

---

[21] Amnesty International (12Aug. 2013 last Accessed.) https://www.amnesty. org/en/who-we-are/about-amnesty-international.

What if Napoleon had not been exiled to the islands of Elba and St. Helena?

Would he have been able to come back as a Kaiser?

What if there was a new volcano on Iceland?

In 2010, the eruption of the Icelandic volcano Eyjafjallajökul had severe implications for individuals and businesses around the world; in particular, many airline companies suffered. The total losses were enormous.

What if China had not built the Great Wall?

The building of the wall started in the fifth century BC; it is more than 6,000 kilometres long. First, the Chinese people at the time would not have had a tax increase of between 10 and 50 per cent. Second, what would all the tourists to China visit without it?

What if the White House had not been rebuilt after the fire in 1814?

The building of the White House started in 1792, and the first fire was in 1814, followed by a second in 1929. Would President Obama be homeless if the White House had not been rebuilt? By the way, it was the English who burned the White House.[22]

What if the spinning machine had not been invented?

The invention of the automatic spinning machine led to the Industrial Revolution.

---

[22] Moen Ole O. USAs Presidenter Fra George Washington til Barack Obama (USAs Presidents) 2009.

What if colonization had never begun?

The colonial countries, like Great Britain, France, Spain, and Portugal, behaved as if they owned the world, with sovereign rights to all natural resources. How many resources and valuables did these countries remove from their colonies?

What if these greedy colonial countries had to pay back what they stole during the colonial period?

What if the colonial period had never ended?

Forget the United States, the European Union, and the Far East. We would have the Great Britain Union, the French Union, the United States Union, the Spanish Union, and the Portuguese Union.

What if Alexander the Great had been defeated at Granikos?

What if the United States had not dropped the atom bomb on Hiroshima and Nagasaki?

What if Napoleon had supported America in 1812?

What if Cleopatra had stayed away from Roman General Antonius?

What if the Romans had defeated the Germanic peoples?

What if Luther had been burned at the stake?

What if Napoleon had not sold Canada?

What if Harold had not won the Battle of Hastings?

What if Napoleon had won the Battle of Waterloo?

What if Japan had not bombed Pearl Harbor?

This attack prompted the United States to enter World War II.

What if Spain had not sold Florida?

When Spain and the United States signed the Adams-Onis Agreement in 1819, Spain agreed to sell it Florida for $5 million. What if Florida were still Spanish? Florida later became the most economically successful state in the country, but that's a long time ago.

What if you could buy Florida for the same price today?

What if British Museum had to return all the stuff they got from abroad?

There are some disputes as several countries argue that the British Museum stole items which do not belong to them as they received this for example during the colony period where Great Britannia behaved as they own the world.

What if Scotland 'divorce from rest of the UK and becomes independent?

Scotland was an independent country from its foundation in the Early Middle Ages (traditionally 843) until 1707, with the Treaty of Union and subsequent. Since then, they have fought for getting their independence back. What would the consequences be?

- It would be an available position as a monarch or a president.
- They would have to establish their own currency or join the EURO.

- They would have to take over part of UKs debt, which is significant.
- They would have to decide whether they would apply for membership in the EU or EEA which might takes a few years.
- The oil and gas resources UK owns have to be split.
- And a lot of other practical matters will have to be solved.

Holidays

What if God had not invented the holiday?

According to the Bible, God created the earth in six days and rested on the seventh. Only one day's holiday? The unions have been able to create more holidays than God.

What if no maps ever had been drawn?

The Greek philosopher Anaximander (610-547 BC) is considered to be the first scientific geographer and cartographer.

What if you could go on a once-a-lifetime holiday?

What if you had to go on holiday with your ex for one month?

Would you talk to each other, fight, kill each other, have sex, or make up and go back to each other?

Home

What if nobody had to sleep on the streets?

What if there was no wallpaper?

The wallpaper industry would probably be bankrupt then.

What if you had a butler?

Many women actually do, like my girlfriend, who has me!

What if you are searching for paradise?

Look at your home.

Humour

What if World Rally Champion Petter Solberg learned English?

In an interview, Solberg said, 'It is not the farts that kills, but the smell.' What he probably meant to say was that it is not the speed that kills, but the accident.

What if Norwegian female football players learned English?

After making a goal in an important match, a player was asked how she managed to score; she said, 'I tried to screw the ball in the corner.' I thought it was a football match, but it seems that they were playing with other balls.

What if we did not have an IQ?

Some people don't, but they work for the government.

What if you need to buy something for somebody who has everything?

Why not give them this book?

What if you went to a foreign country and could not speak a single word of their language?

Would you be able to go the pharmacy and buy a condom using sign language?

Would you be able to buy toilet paper using sign language?

What about aperients, if you had a belly problem?

What if you could repeat the best quote ever?

What if we didn't have any humour?

Some people don't.

What if I have offended somebody with this book?

So what? I have only told the truth, but the truth is sometimes difficult to face.

What if you had an ant up in your bump?

Internet and Computers

What if you lit 7,000 wrapped sparklers?[23]

What if I drilled a tunnel through the centre of the earth and jumped into it?[24]

What if you tried to hit a baseball pitched at 90 per cent the speed of light?[25]

What if . . . you went outside and laid down on your back with your mouth open, how long would you have to wait until a bird pooped in it?[26]

What if . . . a rainstorm dropped all of its water in a single giant drop?[27]

[23]   What would happen if you lit 7000 wrapped sparklers? NatGeo TVUK. (Accessed 12 Aug. 2013.) http://www.youtube.com/watch?v=tOH4GYxGx0Q.

[24]   Gerbis Nicholas. What would happen if I drilled a tunnel through the centre of the earth and jumped into it? HowSstuffWorks. Inc. (Accessed 12 Aug. 2013.) http://science.howstuffworks.com/environmental/earth/geophysics/question373.htm.

[25]   McManis Ellen. What would happen if you tried to hit a baseball pitched at 90 per cent the speed of light? xkcd. (Accessed 12 Aug. 2013.) http://what-if.xkcd.com/1/.

[26]   Olson Adrienne. Ifyou went outside and lay down on your back with your mouth open, how long would you have to wait until a bird pooped in it? xkcd (Accessed 12 Aug. 2013.) http://what-if.xkcd.com/11/

[27]   McNeil Michael. What if a rainstorm dropped all of its water in single giant drop? Xkcd. (Accessed 12 Aug.2013) http://what-if.xkcd.com/12/.

What if . . . my printer could literally print out money, would it have that big an effect on the world?[28]

What if you fired a gun on a train moving as fast as a bullet?[29]

What if the earth stood still?[30]

What if you farted inside a space suit?[31]

According to Astonishing Science Spectacular Museum:

> *"It would be the worst kind of fart ever: you couldn't deny it, you couldn't escape it, and the smell would stay with you all the way back to the space station.*

What if the entire world lived like Americans?[32]

[28] O'Brian Derek. If my printer could literally print out money, would it have that big an effect on the world? Xkcd. (Accessed 12 Aug. 2013.) http://what-if. xkcd.com/23/.

[29] What would happen if you fired a gun on a train moving as fast as a bullet? HowSstuffWorks. Inc. (Accessed 12 Aug. 2013.) http://science.howstuffworks. com/question456.htm.

[30] Fraczek Witold. If the Earth Stood Still. Esri. Understanding the world. (Accessed 12 Aug. 2013.) http://www.esri.com/news/arcuser/0610/nospin. html.

[31] Glenn. What would happen if you farted inside a space suit? Astonishing Science. Spectacular Museum. (Accessed 12 Aug. 2013.) http://www. sciencemuseum.org.uk/onlinestuff/snot/what_would_happen_if_you_ farted_in_a_space_suit.aspx.

[32] What would happen if the entire world lived like Americans? The Change Generation. (Accessed 12 Aug. 2013.) http://www.fastcoexist.com/1680379/ what-would-happen-if-the-entire-world-lived-like-americans.

What if a small black hole hit the earth?[33]

What if you fell into a black hole?[34]

What if everyone on earth jumped at the same time?[35]

What if the United States went back to the gold standard?[36]

What if Greece left the Euro zone?[37]

What if you fell into a volcano?[38]

What if we stopped vaccinations?[39]

[33] O'Neil Brian. What would happen if a small black hole hit the earth? Universe Today. (Accessed 12 Aug. 2013.) http://www.universetoday.com/12837/what-would-happen-if-a-small-black-hole-hit-the-earth/#ixzz295mY05St.

[34] Wolchover Natalie. What would happen if you fell into a black hole? The Huffington Post. (Accessed 12 Aug. 2013.) http://www.huffingtonpost.com/2012/04/13/what-would-happen-if-you-fell-into-a-black-hole_n_1424517.html.

[35] Limer Eric. What would happen if everyone on earth jumped at the same time? Gawker Media (Accessed 12 Aug. 2013.) http://gizmodo.com/5936007/what-would-happen-if-everyone-on-earth-jumped-at-the-same-time.

[36] What would happen if the United States went back to the gold standard? The Week Publications Inc. (Accessed 12 Aug. 2013.) http://theweek.com/article/index/232462/what-would-happen-if-the-us-went-back-to-the-gold-standard.

[37] What could happen if Greece leaves the eurozone? BBC. (Accessed 12 Aug. 2013.) http://www.bbc.co.uk/news/business-18074674.

[38] Wolchover Natalie. What would happen if you fell into a volcano? Discovery Communication LLC. (Accessed 12 Aug. 2013.). http://news.discovery.com/earth/weather-extreme-events/volcano-garbage-waste-lava-burn-video-person-120627.htm.

[39] What would happen if we stopped vaccinations? Centres for Disease Control and Prevention. (Accessed 12 Aug. 2013.) http://www.cdc.gov/vaccines/vac-gen/whatifstop.htm.

What if the Internet collapsed?[40]

What if every single person in the world pointed a laser pen at the moon?[41]

What if we don't recycle?[42]

What if sharks disappeared?[43]

What if the earth stopped spinning?[44]

What if all law enforcement agencies could do instant DNA analysis?[45]

What if an earthquake struck Las Vegas?[46]

---

[40] Strickland Jonathan. What would happen if the Internet collapsed? HowSstuffWorks. Inc. (Accessed 12 Aug. 2013.) http://computer.howstuffworks.com/internet/basics/internet-collapse.htm.

[41] Chan Casey. What would happen if every single person in the world pointed a laser pen at the moon? Gawker Media. (Accessed 12 Aug. 2013.) http://gizmodo.com/5948820/what-would-happen-if-every-single-person-in-the-world-pointed-a-laser-pointer-at-the-moon.

[42] What would happen if we don't recycle? Squidoo, LLC. (Accessed 12 Aug. 2013.) http://www.squidoo.com/recycle-pollution.

[43] Heimbuch Jaymi. What would happen if sharks disappeared? MNN Holding LLC. (Accessed 12 Aug. 2013.) http://www.treehugger.com/ocean-conservation/what-would-happen-if-sharks-disappeared.html.

[44] Odenwald Sten Dr. What would happen if the earth stopped spinning? Dr. Sten Odenwald. (Accessed 12 Aug. 2013.) http://image.gsfc.nasa.gov/poetry/ask/q1168.html.

[45] Messmer Ellen. What if all law enforcement agencies could do instant DNA analysis? NetworkWorld Inc. (Accessed 12 Aug. 2013.) http://www.networkworld.com/news/2012/100412-what-if-security-dna-262971.html.

[46] Shine Conor. What would happen if an earthquake struck Las Vegas? Las Vegas Sun. (Accessed 12 Aug. 2013.) http://www.lasvegassun.com/news/2012/oct/03/city/.

What if an 8.9 quake hit the United States?[47]

What if a lion fought a tiger?[48]

What if you shot a gun in space?[49]

What if the earth stood still for one full minute?[50]

What if the Gulf Stream stopped flowing?[51]

What if type A blood were given to a person who has type B blood?[52]

What if type B blood were given to a person who has type A blood?[53]

[47] Butler Kiera. What would happen if an 8.9 quake hit the United States? Mother Jones and the Foundation for National Progress. (Accessed 12 Aug. 2013.) http://www.motherjones.com/blue-marble/2011/03/what-would-happen-if-89-quake-hit-us.

[48] Wolchover Natalie. What would happen if a lion fought a tiger? Yahoo! Inc. (Accessed 12 Aug. 2013.) http://news.yahoo.com/happen-lion-fought-tiger-112933787.html.

[49] Wolchover Natalie. What if you shot a gun in space? TeckMedia Nework. (Accessed 12 Aug. 2013.) http://www.livescience.com/18588-shoot-gun-space.html.

[50] Brain Marshall. What if the earth stood still for one full minute? HowSstuffWorks. Inc. (Accessed 12 Aug. 2013.) http://blogs.howstuffworks.com/2009/10/26/what-would-happen-if-the-earth-stood-still-for-one-full-minute/.

[51] Johannessen Ola. M. And what would happen if Gulf Stream stopped? Redrawn. (Accessed 12 Aug. 2013.) http://ec.europa.eu/research/rtdinfo/special_pol/04/print_article_2603_en.html.

[52] What would happen if type A blood were given to a person who has type B blood? Answer Corporation. (Accessed 12 Aug. 2013.) http://wiki.answers.com/Q/What_would_happen_if_type_A_blood_was_given_to_a_person_who_has_type_B_blood.

[53] What would happen if type B blood were given to a person who has type A blood? Answer Corporation. (Accessed 12 Aug. 2013.) http://wiki.answers.com/Q/What_would_happen_if_type_B_blood_was_given_to_a_person_who_has_type_A_blood.

What if a person with type B blood was given type O blood?[54]

What if everybody in the United States flushed the toilet at the same time?[55]

What if the ozone layer was destroyed?[56]

What if you peed on an electric fence?[57]

Do not try it!

What if the Hoover Dam broke?[58]

What if you could delete the Internet?

What if you had to read all the e-mails in the world sent in one week?

---

[54] What would happen if a person with type B blood was given type O blood? Answer Corporation. (Accessed 12 Aug. 2013.) http://wiki.answers.com/Q/What_would_happen_if_a_person_with_type_b_blood_were_given_type_o_blood.

[55] Clark Josh. What if everybody in the United States flushed the toilet at the same time? HowSstuffWorks. Inc. (Accessed 12 Aug. 2013.) http://home.howstuffworks.com/home-improvement/plumbing/everybody-flushes-toilets.htm.

[56] What would happen if the ozone layer was destroyed? Answer Corporation. (Accessed 12 Aug. 2013.) http://wiki.answers.com/Q/What_would_happen_if_the_Ozone_layer_was_destroyed.

[57] What would happen if you peed on an electric fence? NatGeo TVUK. (Accessed 12 Aug. 2013.) http://www.youtube.com/watch?v=t0H4GYxGx0Q&list=PLCE4262D88AB2C935.

[58] Neer Katherine. What would happen if the Hoover Dam broke? HowSstuffWorks. Inc. (Accessed 12 Aug. 2013.) http://science.howstuffworks.com/engineering/structural/hoover-dam-broke.htm.

What if you need Adobe Flash Player?

Download it then.

What if you had to pay for using the Internet?

What if you want to share your pictures or videos on Pinterest?

Think about it twice before you submit your private photos or videos.

What if you could get all apps free?

What if you had to read all the blogs on Tumblr?

That would take you some serious time. As of May 19, 2013, Tumblr hosted over 108 million blogs.

What if we did not have USB memory sticks?

The memory stick was patented in 2006 by Chin-Chien Lin.[59]

What if Steve Jobs had not been interested in computers?

Steve Jobs (1955-2011) was the co-founder of Apple Inc. and built the first Apple computer in his garage. Apple products include the Macintosh line of computers, the iPod, the iPhone, and the iPad. In 2013, Apple was the largest public trading company in the world according to market capitalization and the largest technology company in the world by revenue and profit.[60] In 2012, Apple had

---

[59]   Wikipedia
[60]   *Financial Times* Global 500—based list is up to date as of March 28, 2013.

sales of $156,508 billion and more than to 76,000 full time and part time employees, a little bit too large to be in Jobs' garage.[61]

What if you had to live without computers, Facebook, Twitter, or mobile phones?

Your parents probably did, but they are from the Stone Age.

What if your work computer broke down and you did not have a backup?

It happens every day! Some companies might go bankrupt if they lose everything they have saved on computers with no backup.

What if your personal computer broke down and you did not have a backup?

It happens every day! Make sure you back up all the time, and make sure it works.

What if we did not have any search engines like Google, Yahoo, Baidu, Bing, or Ask?

What if we did not have Internet broadband?

The younger generation has grown up with broadband, but it has not always been like this. In the beginning, Internet users had to use slow telephone lines, with no possibility of downloading huge documents, music, or films.

---

[61] Apple Annual Report 2012 http://www.sec.gov/Archives/edgar/data/320193/000119312512444068/d411355d10k.htm.

What if Google Earth could show other people your bathroom and bedroom?

What if you could receive one cent of every payment made on PayPal worldwide?

You would be very rich.

What if the Internet was down for one month?

Would everything stop? Could the banks open, could we fly, could we do business? Could we shop, pay the bills, take out cash, do networking, or travel?

What if we did not have the World Wide Web (www)?

Tim Berners-Lee (1955-present), a computer scientist, came up with the idea of the first web browser and web server when sitting in a café. When he and a colleague suggested to their manager that they should develop it, the manager thought the idea was vague but exciting; fortunately, he let them work on it.

What if you had bought shares in Facebook a few months before it reached its huge success?

What if you had to read all adverts on Craigslist?

The site gets a million unique monthly visitors in the United States alone; it uses more than fifty servers to host over twenty billion page views per month, with over eighty million new classified advertisements each month.

What if we didn't have e-mail?

E-mail has become one of the most efficient ways of communicating.

What if somebody tried to hack into your computer?

Do you have a satisfactory firewall?

What if you could not use e-mail but had to use carrier pigeons instead?

It worked before.

Inventions

What if Alexander Graham Bell had not invented the phone, or more precisely, stolen the idea from others?

There is no single inventor of the telephone, as it was the result of many inventors' work. However, scientist, inventor, and engineer Alexander Graham Bell (1847-1922) took out a patent on it in 1876; therefore, he is considered its inventor. Antonio Meucci (1808-1889) created a device that picked up sound vibrations, which he patented in 1871, but he could not afford to pay the fee, so Bell took over. Elisha Grey invented the modern phone and preregistered the invention at the patent office; Bell was somehow able to receive secret information from an employee at the patent office. Bell and Grey went to the patent office the same day, but Bell registered the patent first, even though he did not have a model of the invention. Bell's patent application was also suspicious, as he described the phone in the margin of one of his other patent applications. Bell was sued more than 600 times, but he won every case. How did he have time to invent anything with 600 lawsuits against him?[62]

What if the mobile phone had not been invented?

The first mobile phone was introduced by Dr. Martin Cooper (1928-present) and Motorola in 1973. Would you cope without it? Some people say they can live without their families and friends for a week or two, but they could not be without their mobile phone for one hour.

---

[62]   Wikipedia

What if nobody had invented the Internet?

The US Department of Defense introduced the Internet in 1969. That is probably the most positive thing the Department of Defense has done—ever.

What if Wilhelm Conrad Roentgen had not discovered X-rays?

In 1895, physicist Wilhelm Conrad Roentgen (1845-1923) detected electromagnetic radiation in a wavelength range known today as X-rays (or Röntgen rays).

What if the wheel had not been invented?

The wheel was probably invented in ancient Mesopotamia (present-day Iraq, Syria, Turkey, and Iran) in the fifth millennium BC or in China around 3,500 BC.

What if Alfred Nobel had not invented dynamite?

Chemist, engineer, innovator, and armaments manufacturer Alfred Nobel (1833-1896) invented dynamite, which was patented in 1876. Was his last act of establishing the Nobel Prize a consequence of a bad conscience?

What if Johannes Gutenberg had not introduced printing?

Blacksmith, goldsmith, printer, and publisher Johannes Gutenberg (1398-1468) introduced printing and was the first to use movable type printing in 1439.

What if Thomas Alva Edison had not invented the light bulb?

Inventor and businessman Thomas Edison (1847-1931) patented the electric light bulb in 1880. It would be very dark without it.

What if Samuel F. B. Morse had not invented the single-wire telegraph system?

Samuel Morse (1791-1872) contributed to the invention of a single-wire telegraph in 1837. Twelve years before, his wife had fallen ill while he was travelling, and he received the message too late. When he returned home, she was dead. Morse then decided to invent a faster means of communication. For a long time, the telegraph was the only method of long-distance communication. In 1859, the American government recognized that they needed a faster means of communication. At that time, there was tension between America and Britain, and when a hungry pig invaded an American's farm to find food, the farmer shot the pig, and both parties started an armaments race. The president of America required a more efficient and quicker way of communication due to the pig that almost started a war between UK and the United States. The telegraph industry got a boost and quickly grew.[63]

What if he had not developed Morse code?

Morse was co-inventor of the Morse code, which was in extensive use from the 1890s. It was vital during World War II and saved a lot of lives.

---

[63]   Illustrert Vitenskap Historie 2012

What if the radio had not been invented?

Several inventors contributed to the invention of the radio, but inventor and mechanical and electrical engineer Nikola Tesla (1856-1943) took out two important patents in 1897. Could you imagine a world without radio?

What if television had not been invented?

Television has been commercially available since the late 1920s; it is the result of many inventors' ideas and improvements. What would parents do on Saturday and Sunday mornings if their children could not watch TV?

What if our forefathers had not found out how to milk cows and goats?

What if spectacles had never been invented?

Probably half of the world's population needs spectacles to read, watch television, or drive. The first spectacles were probably invented in Italy in 1286 by Friar Giordano da Pisa (1255-1311). However, it was not until 1604 that mathematician, astronomer, and astrologer Johannes Kepler (1571-1630) published the first correct explanation as to why convex and concave lenses could correct presbyopia and myopia.

What if the zip had not been invented?

What if the fridge had not been invented?

The modern fridge was invented in 1876 by engineer Carl von Linde (1842-1934).

What if the freezer had not been invented?

Home freezers were introduced in the United States in 1940.

What if lipstick had not been invented?

Would women have survived without it? Eleanor Kairalla patented it in 1944. Try to imagine her fortune even if she got only a one-penny royalty fee for each lipstick sold.

What if car airbags had not been invented?

Allan Breed introduced the airbag sensor for crash detection for Chrysler in 1967.

What if paper or papyrus had not been invented?

It is uncertain when paper was invented, but some suggest it is from the first century AD.

What if nobody had thought of the tampon?

The tampon has probably been around since the eleventh century, but what did women do before that?

What if Marie Curie had not done research on radioactivity?

Physicist and chemist Marie Curie's (1867-1934) discovery resulted in, for example, the successful treatment of cancer.

What if the dishwasher had not been invented?

Josephine Cochrane (1839-1913) invented the dishwasher in 1886. She was a very rich person who never did the dishwashing herself. All men should be thankful to her.

What if the camera had not been invented?

The first photograph was taken in 1822 by Joseph Nicéphore Niépce (1765-1833). The first color film was introduced in 1935, and the digital camera first came on the market in 1991.

What if the camera with roll film had not been invented?

Roll film was patented by innovator and entrepreneur George Eastman (1854-1932) in 1888.

What if the hand axe had not been invented?

The hand axe is the longest-used tool in human history; the first hand axe was developed around 1.5 million years ago (early Stone Age).

What if the telescope had not been invented?

Physicist, mathematician, astronomer, and philosopher Galileo Galilei (1564-1642) appropriated an idea from a spectacle-maker and developed the telescope in 1609.

What if Benz, Daimler, and Ford had not been interested in cars?

Engine designer and car engineer Karl Friedrich Benz (1894-1929) and investor Bertha Benz are regarded as the inventors of the gasoline-powered car; Karl Benz was granted a patent for the first car in 1886. It was Bertha Benz who suggested that the car should have more than one gear. Engineer, industrial designer, and industrialist Gottlieb Daimler (1834-1900) invented the high-speed petroleum engine, while industrialist Henry Ford (1863-1947) was able to produce cars inexpensively with his moving assembly line.

What if the adjustable spanner had not been invented?

Jack Johnson (1878-1946) was the first black person to win boxing's world championship in 1908. He married a white woman, which was unlawful at that time, and he was jailed. In prison, he came up with the idea of the adjustable spanner; he improved a previous version and patented it in 1922.

What if the screwdriver had not been invented?

The first screwdriver was probably in use from around 1400 and was used to adjust and fix suits of armor.

What if the hammer had not been invented?

The hammer has been an important tool for humankind's development. The first very simple version was probably used 2.4 million years ago; 30,000 years ago, some unknown genius got the great idea of using a handle, making the hammer more efficient.

What if the trowel had not been invented?

It is uncertain when the trowel was invented, but it is believed that it was in use during the Roman Empire.

What if the sledgehammer had not been invented?

Stone hammers are known to date back to 2,600,000 BC.

What if ball-bearings had not been invented?

The ball-bearing was first patented in 1869 by Jules Suriray, a bicycle mechanic. The main purpose of a ball-bearing is to reduce rotational friction.

What if the saw had not been invented?

It is believed that the Egyptians used the first saw in 3,000 BC. The first one was probably made of an animal jaw.

What if nobody had ever thought of air conditioning?

Engineer and inventor Willis H. Carrier (1876-1950) thought of this in 1906. Without air conditioning, places like Miami and Orlando would probably be deserted.

What if the battery had not been invented?

Physicist Alessandro Volta (1745-1827) is credited with the invention of the first battery in 1800, but he paid tribute to three other inventors for developing the battery.

What if the microscope had not been invented?

English natural philosopher, architect, and polymath Robert Hooke (1635-1703) created the first compound microscope in 1665.

What if nobody had invented the mirror?

Could women survive without it? Could men? The earliest manufactured mirrors date to around 6,000 BC. The modern silvered-glass mirror is credited to chemist Justus von Liebig (1803-1873) in 1835.

What if nobody had invented radar?

We might not get a fine for speeding, but could you fly without radar? In 2007, the world's busiest airport, Hartsfield-Jackson Atlanta International Airport, had 994,346 landings and takeoffs during the course of one year, which is 2,724 each day, or almost two every minute! That means two takeoffs or landings each minute, every minute, the whole year. Would you be happy to land or take off if there was no radar?

What if we did not have matches?

Physicist Robert Boyle was the first to experiment with making matches in 1680.

What if the bra had not been invented?

What if nobody had invented tape?

What if the umbrella had not been invented?

So what?

What if the pen had not been invented?

What if toilet paper had not been invented?

What if we had to sail without rudders?

Without the rudder, it would be extremely difficult to maneuver a ship. The rudder was in use in ancient Egypt, Rome, and China.

What if the wheelbarrow had not been invented?

It is believed that the first wheelbarrow was in use in ancient Greece and China from the second century. It was probably invented by a lazy worker who did not want to carry everything on his shoulders.

What if farmers did not have an iron plough?

The iron plough greatly reduced the burden of farmers; it was a technical revolution when it was invented.

What if engineers had not been able to build the suspension bridge?

The longest suspension bridge, the Akashi Kaikyō Bridge in Japan, is 1,991 metres long and was built in 1998.

What if there was no ultrasound?

Parents used to have to wait until birth before they could know the sex of their baby.

What if we did not have the compass?

What if the harvester had not been invented?

Law

What if there were no laws, rules, or legislation?

The first known written law is from the eighteenth century BC, when King Hammurabi in Babylon (south of present-day Baghdad) inscribed 282 codified laws on a column of basalt. The laws were retained until 539 BC; probably no other legislation has been in force for so long.

What if there was no copyright?

Copyright is a legal concept giving the creator of an original work exclusive right to it. It refers to intellectual property (IP), which means that nobody can copy or use it without the owner's permission. Without copyright, anyone could use and sell the property, for example, a book, without the author's consent. King Charles II of England was concerned by the unregulated copying of books and passed the Licensing Act of 1662 by Act of Parliament, while the legal concept was implemented in the United States in 1787. The Berne Convention is a treaty governing copyright; owners do not need to register in each country in order to establish the copyright. Some years ago, Walt Disney's copyrights were about to expire, which meant that anyone could have copied Disney's work, including Mickey Mouse. The Disney Corporation strongly lobbied Congress and convinced them that the period for copyright should be extended for another fifty years.

What if businesses could not claim intellectual property rights?

Intellectual property refers to a set of exclusive rights which are recognized and protected. Common types of intellectual property, also called immaterial rights, include patents, trademarks and trade names, copyrights, trade secrets (know-how), and industrial design rights. The British Statute of Monopolies 1623 is now seen as the origin of patent law and the Statute of Anne 1710 as the origin of copyright. Corporations spend billions on developing intellectual property; without its protection, they would not be so interested in making investment.

What if we had no human rights?

What if you broke up with your partner without having a legal agreement?

Who would have the right to your home, your cars, your shares, and your savings? Which of you would be responsible for the debt? Would it be another fight or war between you?

What if you had written an agreement with your partner when you were friends?

Everything would be much simpler if the agreement had been written when you were still friends.

What if the jury system had not been introduced?

Mathematics

What if we did not have mathematics?

Could we have had coped without mathematics? It is believed the first mathematics was used in Africa 33,000 years ago. In 1970, a baboon bone inscribed with some simple mathematics was found in Swaziland in Africa. Would you feel safe if you knew that the captain on a flight from London to Melbourne could not calculate how much fuel was needed?

What if we did not have zero?

Zero has not always existed. It was invented in India around the ninth century, but Europeans were skeptical for several hundred years before they also adopted it. They wondered how nothing can be something. Could you imagine a world without zero today?

What if there were no numbers?

What if we could not use fractions?

Around 1850 BC, the ancient Egyptians started to use fractional arithmetic; they also discovered how to calculate something's area. They needed to calculate all the pharaohs' building projects, like the pyramids, including workers' salaries and tax. The Rhind papyrus from 1850 BC contained eighty-seven mathematical principles, such as multiplication, division, and fractional arithmetic. Many of these principles were used for fundamental mathematics by Greek mathematicians.

What if we did not have equations or square and cube roots?

The Babylonians learned to use equations, square roots, and cube roots in 1800 BC; this was confirmed when the Plimpton 322 clay tablet was found. The clay tablet also suggests that the Babylonians had established methods to find the long side of a rectangular triangle ($a^2 + b^2 = c^2$), which philosopher and mathematician Pythagoras (570-495 BC) was credited for 1,500 years later.

What if we did not have π (pi)?

Pi (π) defines the relationship between a circle's radius and its diameter. In 250 BC, mathematician, physicist, engineer, inventor, and astronomer Archimedes (287-212 BC) defined π as 3.1428, which was only a 0.04 per cent deviation from the modern calculation (an insignificant deviation).

What if we did not have algebra?

Algebra makes it possible to work with figures in equations without knowing their exact values. Mathematician, astronomer, and geographer al-Khwarizmi (about 780-850) developed algebra in 830.

What if the calculation of probability had not been devised?

French writer and gambler Antoine Gombaud (1607-1684) prompted the calculation of probability. In 1654, he lost a game of dice, which really irritated him, and he asked mathematicians Blaise Pascal (1623-1662) and Pierre de Fermat (1601-1667) to find out why he had not won. Pascal and Fermat created the calculation of probability, which was meant for games, but it developed into the field of statistics.

What if insurance companies could not use probability?

How would they be able to calculate premiums for different insurance policies? Premiums are based on a calculation of probability as to whether a situation will happen. The more likely a happening is, the higher the premium, which is reasonable for both the insurance company and the insured customers.

What if . . . you could establish the perfect code?

Is there a perfect code?

What if the Chinese had not discovered arithmetic?

It would be easier for pupils to do mathematics.

What if we did not have calculators?

You would have to use your fingers. The first calculator was probably a counting frame; the modern calculator was not invented until the 1960s.

Music

What if there were no music?

What if Beethoven, Mozart, Strauss, and Vivaldi had never lived?

No classical music?

What if the 1969 Woodstock Festival had not happened?

The Woodstock festival was attended by 500,000 people; it is considered as the most important event in popular music history. The hippie culture was established with the slogan 'Make love, not war'.

What if Elvis Presley had not popularized rock and roll?

What if you had two tickets to the New Year concert in Vienna?

You would probably not be an ordinary person, because ordinary people do not get tickets. The organizer says that you can register for a draw for tickets, but have you ever heard of any ordinary people getting tickets?

What if you had a voice like Tom Jones?

What if you could not download free music?

What if you had to visit all Redbox stores?

Redbox has more than 42,000 stores, so you would probably not have time to watch any of the films they rent.

What if you had a voice like Whitney Houston?

What if Russia had won the European Song Contest with their song 'What If'?

What if Ann-Frid Lyngstad and Benny Andersson and Agnetha Fältskog and Bjørn Ulvaeus had not divorced?

Abba made a breakthrough with 'Waterloo' in the 1974 Eurovision Song Contest; they eventually sold more than 370 million records worldwide. They made records like 'Mamma Mia', 'Dancing Queen', 'Take a Chance on Me', 'I Have a Dream', and 'The Winner Takes It All'. Would they have created more excellent music if they had not split up?

Nature

What if a grizzly bear fought a polar bear?

What if a lion fought a tiger?

Other

What if you make a big mistake?

1) Try to limit the damage as much as possible, as soon as possible.
2) Apologize.
3) Learn from it so that it does not happen again.
4) Say thank you to those who helped you out of our mistake.

Or do what many other people do: deny it is your fault and blame somebody else.

What if you were honored by a mistake?

What if nobody was interested in business?

What if you could not imagine anything?

What if you had to read the Yellow Pages?

What if you could write the front page of the *New York Times* or *USA Today* for one day?

What if there were no competition?

What if you knew the truth?

What if you were driving at 200 kilometres per hour and opened the car door?

What if you could open the windows of an airplane?

What if you take too much of a risk in sports, business, or daily life?

Some do.

What if you could remember all your dreams in the morning?

What if you could understand them?

What if you could live a second life as another creature?

What would you be?

What if you had a million dollars you could give to a charity?

Who would you give it to?

What if teenagers could get a driving license without having a driving lesson?

What if the Red Cross and Red Crescent emblems did not exist?

Where would the Red Cross be without their emblem?

What if there were no ethics?

What if there were no logic?

The great philosopher Aristotle (384-322 BC) is credited for the beginning of logic, as he was the first person to develop a system for reasoning, a way of describing how thought might lead to knowledge.[64]

What if you could live to the age of 150 years?

It might be lonely as all your friends, children, and grandchildren (and perhaps your great-grandchildren) would pass away before you. On the other hand, you would get a lot from your pension plan.

What if there were no hope left?

What if you really messed it up and your friend submitted a video of the episode to YouTube?

What if humankind was not cautious?

What if Confucius had not established guidelines for individual conduct?

Confucius (K'ung-Tze) (551-478 BC) formed complex guidelines for moral, religious, political, and social ideas. He believed that people are responsible for how they treat other individuals and for their own actions. His rules were simple and are still valid. You should do things because they are right and not merely to achieve advantage. You should love others and honor your parents. He also came up with the doctrine, 'Do not do to others what you do not wish them to do to you'. Confucius was probably one of the world's greatest thinkers.

---

[64]   Stengel, Richard. *Time 100 Ideas That Changed the World* (2010).

What if the Nobel committee had not given the Nobel Peace Prize to Liu Xiaobo?

The relationship between Norway and China would not have been damaged. After Liu Xiaobo won the Peace Prize, the relationship between the countries became ice cold. China did not talk to anyone from the Norwegian government, and businesses suffered.

What if there were no bureaucracy?

Norway's biggest property investor and hotel owner, Olav Thon, recently said that bureaucrats should stay at home with full payment because they destroy business. He said that we have bureaucrats that are so evil and arrogant and that they contribute to a dark future for business and countries. By the way, the bureaucrats disagreed with Thon (for some reason, I don't know).

What if there were no Salvation Army?

What if Mother Theresa had not received the Nobel Prize?

What if you could take it to the next level?

What if you cannot find your spectacles, look on your nose

What if you want one persons trust?

Give him or her yours trust first.

Sir Alex Ferguson

People

What if all overweight people ate 30 per cent less food?

How many food shops would close? Would there be enough food for everyone?

What if there were no morality?

What if people had no shame?

What if people could not read?

What if people could not think logically?

Not everyone does!

What if people could not talk?

What if people could not hate?

What if people could not love?

What if people did not have imagination?

What if there were no inventors?

What if we had no enemies?

What if people had no personal hygiene?

What if every person in the world lived five years more?

What if nobody had any problems?

What if people did not have ability to be thankful?

Some don't.

What if we could not smile?

What if we had no interest in other people?

What if there were no communities?

What if people had no trust in each other?

What if we had no right to vote?

What if people could not speak languages?

What if people could not learn to write?

Cave painting was the beginning of writing; the first cave paintings were discovered in France, dating from around 32,000 years ago.

What if people did not have any creative vision?

Would anything have been created?

What if we did not have the ability to apologize?

What if we did not have the ability to forgive?

What if people did not have any interests?

What if there were no free will, including the choice to do right or wrong?

According to the Bible, the first act of free will was the disobedience of Adam and Eve, when they ate the forbidden fruit of the Tree of Knowledge.

What if there were no tolerance?

What if you could help people in need?

You can. There is always somebody that needs help—just look around.

What if all people could live at peace with each other?

What if people did not continually seek knowledge?

What if people had no compassion?

What if people had no confidence?

What if people could have more respect for other people, their possessions, their cultures, their attitudes, and their behavior?

What if some people were less arrogant?

For example, the French.

What if everyone washed their hands after going to the toilet?

You think they do? They don't.

What if you were a mastermind?

Pleasures

What if there were no tax authorities?

It would be happy days for many people.

What if you had no pleasure?

The Greek philosopher Epicurus (341-270 BC) thought the purpose of life was pleasure. According to Epicurus, politics, love, and sex are not pleasures. Epicurus was probably impotent, like many Greek men.

What if we had no hobbies?

What if all games were free?

Some people would not have time for work.

What if it was forbidden to have pets?

What if you could have a date with Justin Bieber?

Sorry, this one should not be under the heading pleasure. Who would like to meet Justin Bieber, anyway?

What if you need to download free computer wallpaper or ringtones?

Try www.zedge.net; they've got more than eight million free downloads.

What if all books were e-books you could read on Amazon Kindle?

What if Instagram had not been invented?

Instagram has more than 100 million users.

What if there were no fun in the world?

What if there were no make-up?

Could women survive without it? Could men? According to the *Telegraph*, 23 November 2011:

On average, men spend eighty-one minutes a day on personal grooming, including cleansing, toning and moisturizing, shaving, styling hair, and choosing clothes.

Women have their beauty regime down to a fine art and get hair, clothes, and make-up done in just seventy-five minutes.

The research, carried out for Travelodge, found that on an average morning men spend twenty-three minutes in the shower, compared to twenty-two minutes for women.

Men spend eighteen minutes on their shaving regime, compared to fourteen minutes for women despite them having to shave legs, armpits, and bikini line.

What if there were no films available?

What if there were no books available?

What if there were no dancing?

What if you could write a book?

What if you see a person without a smile?

Give him or her yours!

What if you have any ideas for the next volume of _What if_?

We have a competition. If you suggest a very good what-if, you will be included in a draw for a nice surprise. Visit _www.whatif.uk.com_ and e-mail your ideas so that we can put them in the next edition.

What if you have a favorite 'What if . . . '?

There is a competition on the web page. People who vote for the best what-if will be included in a draw for a nice surprise. Visit _www. whatif.uk.com_ and e-mail your ideas so that we can put them in the next edition.

What if you have a 'What if . . .' you hate?

There is a competition is on the web page. People who vote for the worst what-if will be included in a draw for a nice surprise. Visit *www.whatif.uk.com* and e-mail your ideas so that we can put them in the next edition.

What if you want to purchase the next edition of *What if . . . ?*

Visit *www.whatif.uk.com* and register; we will send it to you when the new edition is published.

Politics

What if President John F. Kennedy had not been assassinated?

President Kennedy (1917-1963) was shot in Dallas, Texas, in 1963.

What if President Abraham Lincoln had not been assassinated?

President Lincoln (1809-1865) was assassinated in Ford's Theater in Washington DC in 1865.

What if all presidents and senators had been poor?

Would poverty still exist?

What if we did not have democracy?

In the ancient world, people were ruled by kings, pharaohs, or emperors. Today, most developed countries are democratic, but many countries are still ruled by a single person with no democracy.

What if Mao Tse-Tung had not been leader of the Chinese revolution?

What if nobody used their vote?

What if nobody wanted to be a politician?

What if politicians stop telling jokes and tell the truth instead?

What if you could have a chat with the president of the United States of America?

What if the president of the United States of America had a chat with all Americans?

That would be very time consuming.

What if all countries were communist?

What if Margaret Thatcher, the Iron Lady, had not been prime minister?

What if the European Union had never been founded?

The European Union is an economic and political partnership with twenty-seven member countries; it traces its origins from the European Coal and Steel Community and the European Economic Community (EEC), formed by six countries in 1958. Since then, the union has developed into a huge single market, with the euro as the common currency for most of the members. What began as a purely economic union has evolved into an organization spanning all areas, from development aid to environmental policy. The EU actively promotes human rights and democracy and has the most ambitious emission reduction targets for fighting climate change in the world. Thanks to the abolition of border controls between EU countries, it is now possible for people to travel freely within most of the EU. It has also become much easier to live and work in another EU country.[65] The cornerstone of the EU is the four freedoms: free movement of goods, free movement of capital, free movement of services, and free movement of people.

---

[65] Basic information on the European Union: http://europa.eu/about-eu/basic-information/index_en.htm.

What if people knew how much EU cost the taxpayers?

What if the EU were dissolved?

What if NATO had never been founded?

The North Atlantic Treaty Organization (NATO) was founded in 1949 and brings together twenty-eight member states from Europe and North America. Its fundamental purpose is to safeguard the freedom and security of its members through political and military means.

What if the human rights convention had never had been signed?

The European Convention on Human Rights (in force from 1953) is a treaty to protect human rights and fundamental freedoms in Europe. Similar protections are given in the UN's Universal Declaration of Human Rights; Article 1 reads as follows:

> *All human beings are born free and equal in dignity and rights. They are endowed with reason and conscience and should act towards one another in a spirit of brotherhood.*

What if the UN had never been founded?

The United Nations is an international organization founded in 1945 after the Second World War by 51 countries committed to maintaining international peace and security, developing friendly relations among nations and promoting social progress, better living standards and human rights.

What if Silvio Berlusconi had not been prime minister in Italy?

Maybe Italy would have had a prime minister who was more interested in politics than in sex and that paid his taxes.

What if all politicians—or at least some of them—were honest?

What if Sara Palin had become president of the United States?

Can you imagine that?

What if Mitt Romney had become president of the United States?

What if Hillary Clinton becomes the next president of the United States?

Better or worse than Sara Palin? Better or worse than Barrack Hussein Obama?

What if there had been no Watergate scandal?

This scandal began in 1972 and ended with President Nixon's resignation in 1974. The Watergate scandal involved a break-in at Democratic party headquarters; a cover-up, wiretapping, lies, and the conviction and incarceration of forty-three officials. What else do we remember President Nixon for?

What if a politician makes a big mistake?

They do mistakes all the time, without any consequences for themselves.

What if the politicians should lead all the big businesses?

What if all the politicians left their positions and the business leaders would lead the country?

Practical

What if people had not found out that they could use cotton?

What if we did not have newspapers?

What if you need a dictionary?

Buy one or use the Internet.

What if no ships had ever been built?

What if you need a dropbox?

Rent one.

What if there were no nursery schools?

Religion

What if Jesus Christ had lived?

Jesus Christ is believed to have lived from 7 BC to AD 30-36. How could he have lived in 7 BC? Lots of people do not believe he ever lived, as no evidence has ever been found. Did Jesus Christ really live?

What if Jesus Christ had not lived?

What if Jesus Christ returned to the Earth?

He would probably be shocked, and so would we.

What if you met him?

Some think they have.

What if the Bible were true?

What if the Qur'an were true?

What if God and Allah started to fight?

What if God were a woman?

What if the story about Noah's Ark was true?

What if the Bible had not been written?

What if the Qur'an had not been written?

What if we did not have any religion?

What if there were no God?

What if there was a God?

What if you could meet God?

It would probably have been a hell of a long queue.

What if we had no churches?

What if Martin Luther had not disputed the claim that freedom from God's punishment for sin could be purchased with money?

Theologian Martin Luther (1483-1546) disputed the claim that freedom from God's punishment for sin could be purchased with money; in 1597, he nailed ninety-five theses on the church door. His opinion was that salvation is not earned by good deeds, but received only as a free gift of God's grace through faith in Jesus Christ as redeemer from sin. With this, Luther started the Reformation. If he had not, would we still have to pay for forgiveness?

What if you had to live as a monk or nun for one year?

What if the Apostle Paul had not written his letters?

Twenty-five years after the death of Jesus Christ, Paul wrote letters to the world's Christians, saving Christianity from dissolution. His letters are probably the most important letters ever written, and they later became part of the Bible.

What if Hagia Sofia had never been built?

This church in Istanbul was built between 532 and 537; for more than a thousand years, it was the world's largest religious sanctuary. Now a museum, it is still considered one of the world's most impressive buildings.

What if Jesus Christ had not been crucified?

People have believed in this story for more than two thousand years.

What if Mary had not been a virgin?

What if Joseph had had sex with Mary before Jesus was born?

Was Mary a virgin, or did Joseph want an excuse for making Mary pregnant? He blamed God, and nobody ever thought that they had sex before marriage. What a good explanation he came up with.

What if Buddha had not divorced?

Buddha left his wife and his home when he was 29 years old. This because known as the Great Renunciation, the sudden crystallization of his thought and meditation on the lot of man. What a great explanation he came up with for his divorce: the Great Renunciation.

Who do you think came up with the best explanation, Joseph or Buddha?

What if Buddha had stuck to his first decision, namely that he would only be a Buddha for himself?

What if there were only one religion in the world?

What if you had to join the Jehovah Witnesses?

What if the Jehovah Witnesses members did not deny their children blood transfusions?

What an awful thing to do to your own child. They would rather let their children die before letting them have a blood transfusion.

What if Pilate had set Jesus Christ free?

What if Islam had not been founded?

What if people had not been offered tax exemption if they converted to Islam?

Around AD 630, people in the Roman Empire were offered tax exemptions if they converted to Islam; the first great Caliph said all who accepted his religion and prayed his prayers would be relieved of the poll tax.

This was not an offer to choose between Christianity and Islam; it was really an offer to choose between bondage and freedom. According to Charles Adams, the Muslims used taxation to bring converts into their faith; vanquished people were given three choices: death, taxes, or conversion. Further, Adams said that the new tax policy probably brought more converts to Islam than either the sword or the Qur'an.[66]

What if Buddha had not lived?

---

[66] Adams, Charles. *For Good and Evil, The Impact of Taxes, 131-141* (2nd ed., 1999).

What if the Inquisition and the Crusades had never happened?

The Inquisition and the Crusades are part of the dark history of the church; innocent people suffered or were killed because they did not believe in God. The church should be, and probably is, ashamed of this.

What if you could take the DNA of God?

What if Jesus Christ had a child?

What if the child was born outside marriage, as Jesus Christ was?

What if the seven deadly sins did not exist?

Do you know the seven deadly sins? They are lust, gluttony, greed, sloth, wrath, envy and pride.

What if you could prove that God exists?

Royal

What if Princess Diana was still alive?

Diana (1961-1997), Princess of Wales, who died in a car crash in Paris, was probably the most beloved royal person—ever. When she married Prince Charles in 1981, around 750 million people watched the wedding.

What if Crown Prince Edward had not abdicated and married Wallis Simpson?

What if you had been a royal?

Safety

What if there were no insurance companies?

What if there were no health and safety programmes?

What if it was safe to use the Internet?

Science

What if nobody was interested in science?

What if nobody thought about the greenhouse effect and climate change?

Mathematician and physicist Jean Baptiste Joseph Fourier (1768-1830) is credited for the idea of the greenhouse effect.

What if Robert Hooke had not described the laws of motion?

Physicist, mathematician, astronomer, and philosopher Galileo Galilee (1564-1642) hinted about this phenomenon, but natural philosopher, architect, and polymath Robert Hooke (1635-1703) was the first to describe these laws clearly.

What if Benjamin Franklin had not been interested in electricity?

Author, printer, political theorist, politician, postmaster, scientist, musician, inventor, satirist, civic activist, statesman, and diplomat Benjamin Franklin (1706-1790) proved that lightning bolts are enormous electrical sparks; he invented the lightning rod.

What if magnetism had not been discovered?

Physician, physicist, and natural philosopher William Gilbert (1554-1603) realized that the inside of the earth was magnetic, which impacted navigation of the globe and our lives. As a BBC presenter put it:

> To me, magnetism is one the greatest discoveries of all time, because of its impact throughout history on everything from exploring our world to causing the fantastic light shows of the aurora—but also because of its relevance today in developing renewable technologies.[67]

What if electromagnetism had not been discovered?

Electromagnetism is one of the four fundamental interactions in nature, and even if there is no single person who discovered electromagnetism, it was physicist and chemist Hans Christian Ørsted (1777-1851) who made the surprising observation while preparing for a lecture in 1820.

What if radio waves had not been discovered?

In 1865, physicist and mathematician James Clerk Maxwell (1831-1879) first suggested that there were radio waves.

What if oxygen had not been discovered?

Chemist and biologist Antoine Lavoisier (1743-1794) is credited with the discovery of oxygen, even if a few others had suggested this before him.[68]

---

[67] Osman, Jenny. *100 Ideas that Changed the World. Our Most Important Discoveries Selected by Our Greatest Minds*, p. 157 (2011).

[68] *Sur la combustion en général / Considérations générales sur la nature des acides / Méthode de nomenclature chimique / Traité élémentaire de chimie.*

"The discovery of oxygen was a massive breakthrough, not only because it led to our understanding of chemical reaction, but also because it is the very essence of what keeps us alive".[69]

What if we could not measure longitude?

In 1736, carpenter and clockmaker John Harrison (1693-1776) invented the marine chronometer for establishing the east-west position (or longitude) of a ship at sea; before this, ships had to sail along shore to know their bearings. The invention made it far safer to sail and led to more efficient travel.

What if polar explorers could not cope with freezing cold?

Heroes like Ernest Shackleton, Roald Amundsen, Fritjof Nansen, and Robert Scott put their own lives (and those of their employees) at risk in order to explore the North and South Poles.

What if the universe goes on forever?

What if it doesn't?

What if microwaves had not been discovered?

---

[69] Sosabowski Dr. Hal. *100 Ideas that changed the world—Oxygen. The discovery of the gas of life.(2011).*

Sex

What if Adam had been gay?

Would there be any people on the world?

What if Eve had been lesbian?

What if Adam had been impotent?

What if Adam and Eve's children had not engaged in incest?

The only people were Adam and Eve and their children, who were brothers and sisters.

What if condoms had never been invented?

Condoms have been used for several hundred years; the first ones were made of lamb intestine. If everyone started to use the same condom twice, several condom companies would probably go bankrupt. Every second, condoms are probably in use around the world. How many more people would there be on the earth today if condoms had not been invented?

What if you don't use condoms?

What if you put all the condoms in the world on top of each other?

A hell of a lot of people would have to travel very far to get one.

What if you were paid one cent in royalty fee for every condom used in the world?

What if you were impotent?

What if your girlfriend got pregnant?

What if God had not invented sex?

What if you had to be celibate for one year?

What if you could have as much sex as you wanted?

What if your partner or spouse were unfaithful?

What if there were no equality between men and women?

Is there equality between men and women in 2013? I do not think so.

What if you were under 16 years old and got pregnant?

What if you saw a couple through a window having sex in their own bedroom?

What would you do? Would you watch? Would you walk away? Or would you ring the doorbell and ask them if you could borrow a cup of sugar?

What if Viagra had not been invented?

Some people might think this is the most important invention in history.

What if somebody could invent something similar for women?

What if Bill Clinton, Silvio Berlusconi, Dominique Strauss-Kahn, Boris Johnson, Moshe Katsav, John Edwards, Eliot Spitzer, and Arnold Schwarzenegger had a meeting?

What would the agenda be? Would they discuss politics? Or would they do something else?

Bill Clinton (1946-present) did have sex with Monica Lewinsky, he just tried to change the meaning of the word 'sex'. Silvio Berlusconi (1936-present) has been accused of having sex with prostitutes. Dominique Strauss-Kahn (1949-present) is known as the Horny Baboon after trying to rape a journalist and perhaps a housemaid. London Mayor Boris Johnson (1964-present) had to step down as the vice president of the Conservative party in the UK after claims that he had a female lover (he denied it). Former Israeli president Moshe Katsav (1945-present) was jailed for seven years for raping a female colleague and abusing two others senators. Vice president candidate John Edwards' (1953-present) political career ended in 2009 because of revelations that he had an affair that produced a child; this wrecked his marriage and led to a federal indictment on charges of campaign financial fraud. Eliot Spitzer (1959-present) resigned as governor of New York after claims that he patronized a high-profile prostitute ring. Arnold Schwarzenegger had a baby with his housemaid, and his wife, at the same time. Which head were they thinking with?

What if David Letterman had broadcast a talk show with all these politicians?

The King of Talk Shows, David Letterman (1947-present), claimed that a CBS News employee tried to blackmail him for $2 million by exposing the sexual affairs he had with female subordinates. If he had invited the above mentioned politicians to a talk show, what do you think the topic would be? The topic, of course, would be politics.

What if you could live out your sexual fantasies?

Would you?

What if your partner faked an orgasm?

Would you notice? Would you care?

What if you had to be gay or lesbian for a year?

What if your mum or dad had been infertile?

It would have meant bad luck for you.

What if a stranger asked you whether you would have sex with him or her?

What if the stranger was of the same sex as you?

What if it was forbidden to fake orgasm?

What if our knees had bended the other way? Would men then had to sit on their . . . . and the female on their . . . . instead of on their bump?

What if you agreed on a blind date for having sex, and the blind date turns out to be a close family member?

This has actually happened. According to Orange News[70]:

"A Chinese man met his own daughter-in-law on a blind date in a hotel bedroom after both of them lied about their real names and sent pictures of different people. The woman's husband had suspected his wife on cheating and followed her to the hotel where he found the pair before attacking them. The husband watched his wife enter a hotel bedroom before she changed into a pink bathrobe and headed to another room at Heilongjiang province in northeast China. When she rang the doorbell and his dad answered, the husband flipped out, beating up both of them before police broke up the fight. The old man had lost his job and started chatting online to new people including a woman who he had developed a friendship with—unaware that it was his daughter-in-law and the mother of his grandchild. The daughter-in-law in turn was bored at home being a housewife.

The old man said "We eventually agreed to meet for a romantic liaison, but when I opened the door I don't know if she was more surprised or me. She turned round and ran off down the hallway straight into her husband, my son, who had been following her. He started shouting and then he attacked her, and then he attacked me."

The husband was detained for five days after knocking out two of his wife's teeth and causing his father to be taken to hospital with a head injury."

---

[70]   Orange News, *Man meets daughter-in-law on blind date.* http://web. orange.co.uk/article/quirkies/Man_meets_daughter-in-law_on_blind_date. *25.10.2013*

The moral is, never go on a blind date, unless you know the person you will date.

Who was worst; the old man who were about have sex with his daughter-in-law, the daughter-in-law who cheated on her husband with her father-in-law or the husband who spied on his wife and then knocked down both his father and his wife?

Social Networking

What if we did not have social networking?

What if Facebook had not been introduced?

Facebook is a social networking service and website, founded by computer programmer Mark Zuckerberg (1984-present), Eduardo Saverin (1982-present), Dustin Moskovitz (1984-present), and Chris Hughes (1983-present). Facebook was launched in 2004, and they had more than 1.3 trillion (that's 1,300,000,000,000, or 1.3 million) page views in May 2013. During twenty minutes on Facebook:[71]

- 1.3 million tagged photos
- 1.5 million event invitations
- 1.6 million wall posts
- 1.8 million status updates
- 1.97 million friend requests
- 2.7 million photos uploaded
- 10.2 million comments
- 4.6 million messages

Total number of Facebook users: 1.11 billion

Daily active Facebook users: 665 million

---

[71] Rao Leena. What 20 Minutes On Facebook looks like. 31 Dec. 2010. (12 Aug. 2013 Accessed) http://techcrunch.com/2010/12/31/what-20-minutes-on-facebook-looks-like-1m-shared-links-2-7m-photos-uploaded-10-2m-comments/.

Total number of Facebook mobile users: 751 million

Total number of Facebook friends: 150 billion

Total number of Facebook likes: 1.13 trillion

What will it be like in ten years? Could you manage without it? I could, because I don't even know how to log in.

What if Twitter had not been introduced?

Twitter is an online social network created and launched in 2006 by software architect Jack Dorsey (1976-present). In 2011, it generated over 200 million tweets and handled over 1.6 billion search queries per day.

What if you had to be without a computer, laptop, Facebook, Twitter, mobile phone, texts, i-Pod, Yahoo messenger, and Snapchat for three months?

Would you survive?

What if Facebook users knew how much information Facebook saves about each of them?

When a 24-year-old student asked for copies of information Facebook had saved about him, he received 1,222 pages, even though he had only used Facebook for three years. The file contained messages he had deleted and private information he had never submitted to Facebook.[72] As expected, Facebook denies that they save such information, but how could they send him 1,222 pages if they did not save anything?

---

[72]   *Dagens Næringsliv*, 26 May 2012.

What if you could delete Facebook and Flickr?

So what? Employees would probably start to work again.

What if you become dependent on Facebook?

A psychologist working at a university in Norway believes that some people have a compulsive and excessive relationship; they are dependent on Facebook. Her opinion is that these people might need behavioral therapy and motivational talks with psychologist. Who need a psychologist when you have Facebook?

What if everyone stopped wasting time using social media?

The use of social media is increasing rapidly. How much time are people using on social media during working hours and in their leisure time? Can you imagine if these users spent only five minutes a week on social media? What if they spent five minutes each day?

Number of users in millions[73]

Apple GameCenter	200	Aviary	50	Badoo	170
Camera360	100	Classmates.com	55	Disqus	100
Douban	100	Dropbox	100	E-bay	100
Evernote	60	Facebook	1,110	Flickr	87
Flipboard	56	Gmail	425	Google	343
Google Chrome	750	Gree	190	iCloud	300
Imgur	56	Instagram	100	iQiyi	200
iTunes	500	Kakao Talk	90	Kik Messenger	50

---

[73] "How many people use the top social media, apps, and service," June 2013. (12 Aug. 2013 Accessed) http://expandedramblings.com/index.php/resource-how-many-people-use-the-top-social-media.

Line	150	LinkedIn	225	Living Social	70
Mxit	50	MyHeritage	75	MyLife	60
Netlog	84	Nimbuzz	150	ooVoo	75
Ortsbo	212	Outlook.com	400	Pandora	200
Paypal	123	QQ	825,4	Qzone	611
Reddit	69,9	Renren	178	Ravio (Angry Birds)	1,700
Shazam	300	Sina Weibo	503	SkyDrive	250
Skype	280	SlideShare	50	Socialcam	56
Sonico	55	Soundlound	180	SoundHound	130
Steam	50	Tagged	330	Tango	100
Tumblr	216,3	Twitter	500	Viadeo	50
Viber	200	VK.com	190	Voxer	70
WeChat/ WeiXln	400	WhatsApp	200	WorldPress	66
Yahoo Mail	281	Yelp	100	Youku Tudou	150
YouTube	1,000	Fewer than 50 million users[74]	2,572	TOTAL USERS ON SOCIAL MEDIA	18,830 trillion

[74] App.net, App.net, Biip.no, Blipparm, Buffer, Cloob, Couple, Fitocracy, Groove, HealthTap, Kleii, Airbnb, Bang with friends, Banjo, Cooliris, DXY, eToro, GetGlue, Jiepang, GitHub, Glympse, Gogobot, Habbo Hotel, Hike, Hoppr, Hule Plus, AppGratis, Cubie, Eskimi, Fancy, Feedly, Freelancer, Hootsuite, Hyves, Instapaper, iwiw, iWork, Keek, Kiwibox, LevelUp, Listia, List. ly, LoginRadius, Mailbox, MeetMe, MeetMoi, Mega, MessageMe, NewsHunt, Nexopia, Noom, Ookbee, Openstreetmap, Path, Phhed, Picmix, Plurk, Pocket, Popcornflix, Quora, Rally.org, Ravelry, Bebo, Box.net, Branchout, Busuu, Care2, Change.org, ChatRandom, Deezer, DeviantArt, Edmodo, Etsy, Fab, Flixster, Fotolog, Fotopedia, foursquare, Friends Reunited, Gaia online, Glassdoor, Goodreads, Groupon, iHeartRadio, Kiloo, Last.fm, Life360, LockerDome, Min.com, Mobage, Momo, Mixi, MyFitnessPal, MySpace, Netflix, Odnoklassniki, Pinterest, Prezi, Pulse, qeep, Springpad, Square, Storybird, Stumbleupon, Tango card, Tibbr, Trello, Truecaller, Trulia, Tuenti, Viddy, Viewster, Viggle, Viki, Vimeo, Voddler, Voto, ResearchGate, Rounds, Runkeeper, Saavn, Scoop it, ShopAdvisor, Shopkick, SkillPages, Skyrock, Slacker, Small demons, SnapChat, SnapDeal, Songza, Spotbros, Spotify, Wanelo, Wayn, Waze, Whisper, Wix, WorldFloat.com, Wrapp, Wunderlist, Xing, yammer, Yandex.fotki, Yummly, Zalo, Zing and Zoo.gr.

That's 18.83 trillion (18,830,000,000,000) social media users! If each of these people spent just ten minutes during working hours on social media every day, it would cost employers billions of dollars in salary and lost income.

Space

What if no countries had spent money on space programs?

What is the point of sending a few men to the moon, out in space, or to Mars? Is it wasted money? It costs billions of dollars. What is the benefit, except for the astronauts who get their once-in-a-lifetime holiday?

What if these space nations had spent the money on poverty instead?

What if the Star of David symbol did not exist?

Sport

What if South European football players started to play football instead of acting?

How many penalties and free kicks have they had due to their acting? How many matches have they won due to their acting? Hundreds? Thousands? All of them? Are these players members of the South European Acting Association? Which south European footballer do you think is the Actor of the Year?

What if God's hand had not scored in the World Cup quarterfinal in 1986?

Diego Maradona scored in the quarterfinal in 1986 between England and Argentina, using 'the hand of God'. Argentina won 2-1, and they later beat Germany, 3-2, in the final. What would have happened if Maradona had not cheated and scored with his hand? Nobody knows—maybe England would have made it to the final and won the whole tournament. However, English football fans consider Diego Maradona as the world's biggest cheat and loser, ever, and they will not forgive him in a billion years.

What if no sports were allowed?

What if ESPN had started with a real sport like football instead of baseball?

What if there were no Olympics?

The Olympic Games began in 776 BC in Olympia, Greece, and lasted until AD 393. The International Olympic Committee (IOC) was founded in 1894 when the modern Summer Olympics started. However, the first Winter Olympics were not held until 1924. There were only 258 participants (and perhaps 287 spectators) in the opening ceremony of the first Winter Olympics.

What if no sportsmen were doped?

What if the International Olympic Committee (IOC) had to pay tax?

Before IOC grants a nation to organize the Olympic Games, they require full tax exemption. Is that fair that one of the world's most wealthy organizations shall not pay tax?

Stupidity

What if Starbucks had helped the victims of 9/11?

On September 11, 2001, some ambulance employees in New York City asked a nearby Starbucks for water to treat Ground Zero shock victims; they were charged for $130 for three cases of water! When the ambulance employees later complained to corporate management, it fell on deaf ears. Only after the story appeared in the newspaper did the ambulance company get a refund and an apology from Starbucks' president. Shame on you, Starbucks! I noticed a really bad taste in Starbucks coffee after this episode, and I will never drink Starbucks coffee again. You should not either. Why increase the shareholders' huge fortune even more after this?

What if you could fly around the world without having to tank up the airplane?

What's the point? Paying perhaps $10,000, departing on airport and arrive at the same airport 24 hours later?

Tax

What if no taxes, VAT, or duties were paid to governments?

Would we have schools, hospitals, police, fire brigades, and roads (or would they be only for the rich)?

What if no taxpayer had evaded tax?

Nobody knows exactly how much tax is evaded each year, but according to the Tax Justice Network:

> *The fight against tax havens is one of the great challenges of our age.* [They estimate that] *the amount of funds held offshore by individuals is about $11.5 trillion—with a resulting annual loss of tax revenue on the income from these assets of about $250 billion.*

Cebula and Feige estimate the 2008 US tax gap in the range of $450 to $500 billion, and unreported income to be approximately $2 trillion.[75] During the last two years, more than 100,000 tax evaders have been identified in more than twenty countries. These actions have drawn in 14 billion Euros ($19 billion).[76]

---

[75] Cebula, Richard, and Edgar Feige. *America's Underground Economy: Measuring the Size,* Growth *and Determinants of Income Tax Evasion in the US* (2011).

[76] *International Tax Review.* "Tax Evasion Clampdown Draws in € billion, Says OECD," 26 October 2011.

What if nobody evaded tax at all?

How much would the general tax rate be reduced? 25, 50 or 70 per cent? Nobody knows how much tax is evaded worldwide. I would guess that the tax rate could be reduced to around 10 per cent.

What if all tax inspectors set a good example and did not evade tax?

You don't think they evade tax? Most of them don't, but some do!

What if the mafia boss Al Capone had not evaded taxes?

The police were after Al Capone (1899-1947) for years (at least those in the justice system who were not corrupt and did not accept bribery), and they never succeeded in getting anything on him, even though he ordered the liquidation of hundreds of people. Capone was dedicated to bootlegging liquor, smuggling, and other illegal activities such as prostitution. Despite his criminal record, the police were not able to convict him; the police had to call in the Internal Revenue System, who were finally able to convict Capone of tax evasion and jailed him for eleven years.

What if the Boston Tea Party had never happened?

The Boston Tea Party (1773), a protest against tea taxes, was a key event at the start of the American Revolution. Would the United States have been independent in 1776 without the Tea Party, or would it have continued as a British colony?

What if the Greeks had not evaded tax?

"Evasion of tax in Greece has almost become a national sport. Greece does not have a modern tax system, and taxpayers have nothing to lose with tax evasion. The risk of being caught is minimal. Conservative estimates suggest that tax evasion in Greece is between 5 and 10 billion Euros, or around one-third of the total tax income. Taxpayers consider government employees and politicians as a bunch of thieves who only put tax in their own pockets. It is a total lack of trust between the government and citizens".[77]

George Mavraganis, Tax Manager KPMG Greece

What if you had a tax investigation or a tax raid?

What if the tax office paid you a million dollars by mistake?

What if you could receive your salary tax free for one year?

Many people do—legally—but they might have to move from their home country.

What if taxpayers did not have any legal rights?

Do they actually have any?

What if the tax authorities trusted taxpayers instead of accusing them of cheating and evasion?

That would be great.

What if tax inspectors, or at least some of them, understood tax law?

You should call the newspaper. They might pay you for such news.

---

[77] *Dagens Næringsliv,* July 11, 2011.

What if Mitt Romney had become president of the United States?

Would everyone in the United States start to pay tax? Or would he start to pay a decent tax?

What if you could bribe a tax inspector and then have your income tax-free for life?

How much would you pay?

What if no tax inspectors accepted bribery?

Actually, lots of tax inspectors have been jailed for receiving bribes.

What if the tax authorities around the world start to do the job they are expected to do?

Millions of Americans exist in an underground economy (also called black economy or shadow economy) that has ballooned to $2 trillion annually. One trillion is 1,000,000,000,000. By 'underground economy', we mean all the business activity that is not reported to the government.[78]

What about the rest of the world? In 2009, the OECD concluded that half of the world's workers (almost 1.8 billion people) were employed in the shadow economy, and they predicted that by 2020, the shadow economy would employ two-thirds of the world's workers.[79] The rest of them will probably work for the tax authorities. The underground economy is gigantic. Where are the tax authorities

---

[78]   Patalon Bill. "What America's 2 Trillion Underground Economy Says About Jobs," *Money Morning*, 29 Apr. 2013.

[79]   Rabinowitz Marco. "Rise of the Shadow Economy: Second Largest Economy in the World". *Forbes*. 11 July 2011.

around the world? And what are they doing? Are they doing their job when there are trillions of un-taxed dollars around?

What if the tax authority assesses you wrongly and claim that you to pay?

It happens—too often. How fair is that? The tax authorities pretend that they are fair, that they do the right things that they understand the tax law, that they accept the human rights, but they don't. It seems to me that they don't care as long as they got their monthly pay slip.

What if we could do something about this?

What if you call the tax authority and ask for an advice and they give you wrong advice which you count on?

They will of course deny that they have given wrong advice and you will be responsible and have to face the consequences and pay the tax.

Time

What if the clock had not been invented?

You would never be late for any appointment; you would never know when you had to be at the airport; you would not be late for work; and you would not know when to finish work in the afternoon.

What if all countries in the world had the same time?

Tools

What if we had no filing system?

Not everyone does.

Travel

What if you have to travel by national railway?

Poor you! You need to be prepared: seats are not always available; the trains are dirty; it is very expensive; and the train will probably be delayed, if indeed it turns up at all.

What if you could afford to take a holiday for one year?

What if we could not travel anywhere?

What if the railway had not been invented?

In 1804, the first roadworthy steam locomotive was invented by inventor and mining engineer Richard Trevithick (1771-1833). However, George Stephenson (1781-1848) is considered to be the father of railway with his Rocket train, which reached an amazing speed of 19 kilometres per hour. People were worried and thought that such speed would damage their bodies as well as their sight; they thought that animals close to the railway would die of shock.[80]

What if there were no public transports?

---

[80]   Wikipedia

What if there were no hotels or bed and breakfasts?

The first kind of such accommodation was when some people needed to find another income and started to rent out a room to travelers.

What if there were no traffic lights?

What if you could travel to the moon?

What if you had to live in Greenland for one year?

What if we had no roads?

What if you could cure your fear of flying?

What if you could travel into space?

What if you had no passport?

What if Rio de Janeiro did not have the carnival?

What would Rio be without it?

What if Orlando did not have Disney World, Sea World, Epcot, and all the other theme parks?

What if the Caribbean didn't have its beaches?

What if the Caribbean didn't have tax havens?

What if there were turbulence while you are flying?

So what? It is not dangerous, only unpleasant. If you are wearing a seat belt, the worst that might happen is that that you will spill your coffee or tea.

What if lightning strikes your boat?

What if lightning strikes your aeroplane?

Probably nothing, except that it will be unpleasant and you will be scared, but aeroplanes are built to take it. It happens sometimes, and nobody has died from it.

What if you had to live in the jungle for one month?

Do you think you would survive?

What if you were on a twelve-hour flight in economy class and had to sit between two really overweight people?

What if they also had bad body odour?

What if there were no taxis in London?

You would have to take the tube or walk. Did you know that it takes four years on average to train as a London taxi driver? The drivers need to learn 320 routes, 25,000 streets, and 20,000 landmarks. Still want to be a taxi driver? Why not just buy a GPS? That would be much simpler than spending four years on a scooter driving around London.

What if boats did not have sails?

What if you travel abroad and get sick without having travel insurance?

You might not be treated by foreign doctors in a foreign hospital. If you are treated, you might end up bankrupt if you have to pay for everything yourself.

What if American immigration and passport officers were service minded?

Have you ever travelled to the United States? If so, you would have seen thousands of travellers queuing in front of three desks. When you are finished with passport control, you need to queue for the immigration authority and wait even longer. If you are lucky enough to find a person from passport control or the immigration authority and tell them that you are on a connecting flight and you need to go to the front of the queue, they just look at you. If they do not ignore you, they will tell you that there are a few thousand other travellers that are in transit and will lose their flight as well—so what? If you haven't been to the United States, don't go there unless you can spend a whole day in passport immigration control, giving your fingerprints, scanning your eyes, and so on. The next thing will probably be that you need to give blood and urine samples and show them your bank statements for the last twelve months before they let you in (you may even need to pay a big deposit).

What if you saw an American immigration or passport officer smiling?

You should call the newspaper. They might tip you for such news.

What if you ended up on a deserted island and could take one person with you?

Who would it be?

What if you ended up on a deserted island and could take only one book with you?

Which one?

What if London did not have Big Ben?

Big Ben is one of the most prominent symbols of both London and England; it was finished in 1858. The tower is 96.3 metres tall, 3.3 metres higher than the Statue of Liberty.

TV and DVD

What if LCDs had not been discovered?

Liquid crystal displays (LCDs) are found in mobile phones, flat screens, laptops, GPS devices, and wristwatches. In 1888, botanist and chemist Friedrich Reinitzer (1857-1927) noticed that cholesterol from a carrot had a strange attribution and reflected light in an interesting way.[81]

What if Hollywood had never been established?

In that case, would we have any films at all?

What if Sir David Attenborough had accepted the offer to become a BBC director?

Some years ago, Sir David Attenborough was offered a position as a BBC director, but he refused. What if he had accepted? Would we have had all his nature programs?

What if you had to watch all films on Netflix and Hulu?

Netflix has a collection of 100,000 titles on DVD, so you would need plenty of time.

What if you need to download videos?

You could use YouTube's downloader.

---

[81]   Ibid

Unthinkable

What if there were no corruptions or bribery in the world?

Illicit financial flows, including corruption, bribery, theft, and tax evasion, cost developing countries $1.26 trillion per year, which is equivalent to the economies of Switzerland, South Africa, and Belgium combined. This amount of money could lift the 1.4 billion people living on less than $1.25 a day above this threshold for at least six years.

Source: Global Financial Integrity, 2011.

Over twelve months, one in four people paid a bribe when they came into contact with one of nine institutions and services, from health to education to tax authorities.

Source: Transparency International's Global Corruption Bureau, 2010, surveying 91,500 people across eighty-six countries.

In South Africa, 27 per cent of principals never receive their budgets on time. In Cameroon, half of state primary schools have problems with their buildings: only 19 per cent of schools have working toilets, and barely 30 per cent have enough tables and benches for students.

Source: Transparency International.

Assets placed by wealthy private individuals in tax havens represent an estimated annual loss of roughly $255 billion in tax revenues.

Source: NORAD's 2009 report on tax havens and development.

Countries with weak governance, control of corruption, or rule of law have a 30 to 45 per cent higher risk of civil war.

Source: World Bank World Development Report 2011

More than a third of international business managers estimated corruption increases international project costs by more than 10 per cent, while one-sixth believed corruption inflates costs by more than 25 per cent.

Source: Control Risk and Simmons & Simmons, 2007

What if we had no worries?

How wonderful would that be? Remember what Mark Twain once said:

> *"I've had a lot of worries in my life, most of which never happened."*

How often have you been worried and had the worries come to reality?

What if Hitler had been born a Jew?

What if there were no alarm clocks?

Someone would be happy—and probably late for work every day.

What if Henry Ford had not invented the moving assembly line?

Industrialist Henry Ford (1863-1947) introduced the moving assembly line in 1913 in order to cut manufacturing costs and deliver cheaper cars. His 1908 Model-T Ford cost $825 new; the price dropped to $290 in 1916 (equivalent to $3,289 2011 US dollars).

What if we could buy such cheap cars today?

We cannot, because most governments add 100 per cent or more in taxes and VAT when you buy a new car.

What if there never had been any wars?

How many people would there be on the earth today? Too many?

What if there are living creatures on other planets?

Studies of unidentified flying objects (UFOs) have established that the majority of UFO observations are misidentified conventional objects or natural phenomenon, but between 5 and 20 per cent of reported phenomena remain unexplained.

What if these creatures existed and visited the Earth?

What if you met them?

What if there were no calendars?

What if had to live without all the apps?

Could you manage without Google Maps, WhatsApp Messenger, Facebook Messenger, Gmail, Fruit Ninja, Street View on Google Maps, Voice Search, Google Play Books, Google Play services, Tiny Flashlight, and all the other apps? Your parents survived without all these apps, but they probably do not know what an app is.

What if I-Tunes had not been invented?

What if you were born old and got younger ever day?

You would start your life as rich and retired, and you would become poorer every day. Your life would end with a great orgasm.

What if there were no oil or gas?

Oil and gas are the veins of all industry and transport. How much oil and gas is needed every day worldwide? It is an enormous number of barrels. How long will it last? One year? Ten years? A hundred years?

What if the credit card had never been invented?

The modern credit card was introduced by businessmen Frank B. Namara and Ralph Shneider, who founded Diners Club in 1950 (they probably went to a restaurant and forgot their wallets, so the idea of a credit card came up). Today, the credit card business earns an enormous amount of profit.

What if all people in the world were vegetarian?

Would there be enough food for everyone? Think about all the food the animals we will eat need. Those fields could be used for producing vegetarian food instead.

What if slavery still existed?

Or does it still exist, but in another form? There is still human trafficking, sex slaves, debt slaves, slaves of spouses, and slaves of employers; some children may think they are slaves of their parents when they are asked to clean their room. Pennsylvania was the first US state to end slavery in 1777, only one year after independence.

Slavery in the South did not end until after the American Civil War (1861-1865).

What if there never had been any poverty in the world?

How many people would there be on the earth today? Poverty is perhaps the reason for most deaths.

What if there had never been any wars, dictators, diseases, poverty, and condoms?

The earth would be very crowded then.

What if all drinking water in the world was polluted?

Lots of people still have to drink polluted water, as there is no other alternative.

What if you were president of the United States?

What if there were no football on TV?

What excuse would you use for drinking beer with your friends? Perhaps, you would have to do cleaning instead, so we should be very glad that Cambridge University established modern football.

What if people stopped caring?

What if there were no floods or low tides?

What if you owned the Internet?

What if the North Pole melted?

What if all nuclear power stations in the world were closed on the same day?

What if nobody had invented the alphabet?

Around 5000 BC, the Chinese began to use pictograms and pictures for words, while the Egyptians used hieroglyphs around 3400 to 3200 BC. The oldest known alphabet appears to have been introduced in central Egypt around 1800 BC. There are different alphabets today, like Chinese, Hebrew, Greek, Korean, and Arabic, but the single most widely used system of letters is Latin.

What if no natural resources existed?

What if you were sleepwalking and woke up naked in a crowded place?

What if you could not give your child food or medicine for a month?

Not everyone can!

What if you had to be without your car for two months?

What if sugar had not been discovered?

What if there were a new Ice Age?

What if there were no borders between countries?

What if there were no gold?

What if Nessie, the Loch Ness monster, were found?

What if aliens invaded the Earth?

What if there were no sewer systems?

What if your child used drugs?

What if you were super famous?

What if there were no soap?

What if we did not have any electricity?

What if a tsunami hit your neighborhood?

The most devastating tsunami in modern times was the 2004 Indian Ocean earthquake and tsunami, which killed around 230,000 people in fourteen different countries. The tsunami inundated coastal communities and affected millions of people; a huge number lost all their belongings and homes. The tsunami created a thirty-metre-high wave.

What if Great Britain did not have any pubs?

It would be a crisis, as many Englishmen have their pints during lunch time, after working hours, in the evening, or even before breakfast. Did you know that there are around 54,000 pubs in Britain? *The Guinness Book of World Records* lists Ye Olde Fighting Cocks in St. Albans as the oldest pub on the island, claiming it opened in the eighth century. Old Ferryboat in Holywell claims to have opened in 560, but they can only prove its existence since 1100. Nobody can imagine how many pints Englishmen have consumed since the first pub opened.

What if people did not have any memory?

What if people did not have the ability to recognize?

What if we did not have the ability to concentrate?

What if you had no shoes?

What if it was forbidden to be out in the countryside?

What if there were no humanitarian organizations?

What if there were no volunteers?

What if you could save the life of a murderer?

What if Sir Alex Ferguson had not stepped down as a manager for Manchester United?

He was the longest serving manager of one football club: twenty-five years. He led the club to thirty-seven titles, and the club has 333,000,000 supporters worldwide. There is no one above or beside him. Almost 5 per cent of the world's population supports Manchester United. MU's brand name is probably the most valuable sport club brand in the world.

What if your home burned down?

What if your home was flooded?

What if you could marry an unhealthy 90-year-old billionaire?

Some do!

What if you did and he or she disinherited you?

What if you found a suitcase with one million dollars in cash inside?

Would you keep it?

What if you spent it and the owner turned up?

What if (or when) Prince Charles becomes king of Great Britain?

What if Camilla Parker Bowles became queen of Great Britain?

What a terrible thought.

What if the French could for once produce some good wine?

What if casinos were forbidden in Las Vegas?

Las Vegas would be bankrupt.

What if Churchill had lost power in 1940?

What if the Ottoman Empire had won the Battle of Vienna?

What if the North had lost the American Civil War?

What if Japan had won the Battle of Midway?

What if the Normandy landing on D-Day had not succeeded?

Would the outcome of World War II have been different if the Allied invasion of Normandy not succeeded?

What if you could call God?

The phone operator would probably charge you a fortune.

What if Jesus Christ called you?

Would you put him on hold?

What if it was a reversed charge call?

What if you owned the football team you support?

What if the Coca-Cola Company had been honest and told consumers what Coca-Cola actually contains?

Is there something in Coca-Cola that the company does not want consumers to know about?

What if the sun overslept for a few hours one morning and did not rise?

You should be worried unless you also overslept.

What if females could start listening on males?

What if there was no freedom of speech?

Some places it isn't.

What if *ξωא ҖÇçڿ↓ڵ¥?

What if the globe started to spin slower?

Would we have more than 24 hours each day then?

USA

What if you could unplug Big Brother in USA?

What if some country or EU challenged US or their jurisdiction to do surveillance abroad?

What if USA could be trusted a country again?

What if USA could achieve the same reputation and respect they had before Edward Snowden published the truth?

What if all countries that have been spied on by USA had spied on USA?

What if Angela Merkel all the other country leaders that have been spied on had spied on Barack Obama?

What if National Security Agency (NSA) had to public all their files and methods?

They don't need to—Edward Snowden has done it for them. Or perhaps Snowden only knew a small part of what actually is going on in NSA.

What if NSA is spying on Barack Obama?

John Edgar Hoover in FBI spied on everyone, probably also the president. So have anything changed since then?

What if NSA infiltrates links to Yahoo, Google data centers worldwide?

According to a report published by Washington Post they do[82]:

> "*The National Security Agency has secretly broken into the main communications links that connect Yahoo and Google data centers around the world, according to documents obtained from former NSA contractor Edward Snowden and interviews with knowledgeable officials.*"

What if USA had respected human rights and people's privacy and stopped spying in secrets on their citizens, their alliance and friend, other country leaders?

What if everyone in the USA who had been spied on had left USA?

Would it have been anyone left?

What if every person and countries in the world that have been spied on had terminated all their connections with USA?

What if you start to criticize USA and NSA in public?

What if NSA could respect their own privacy policy?

---

[82] Washington Post, *NSA infiltrates links to Yahoo, Google data centers worldwide, Snowden documents say,* 30.10.2013. Available at http://www.washingtonpost.com/world/national-security/nsa-infiltrates-links-to-yahoo-google-data-centers-worldwide-snowden-documents-say/2013/10/30/e51d661e-4166-11e3-8b74-d89d714ca4dd_story.html?hpid=z1. Last visited 31.10.2013.

According to their web page[83]:

> *"NSA is committed to protecting your privacy and will collect no personal information about you unless you choose to provide that information to us."*

This was very satisfactory; I did not thought that they asked you before they collected personal information. Did they ask Angela Merkel and the other state leaders?

What if you visit NSA's home page?

According to their web page:

> *The National Security Agency Web site automatically logs visitor information concerning the pages read, photographs viewed, and information downloaded for statistical purposes.* **This information does not identify you personally.** *The information gathered helps us to assess the content most interesting to visitors and to determine technical design specifications for identifying system performance issues. The following represents the types of information automatically collected and stored about your visit:*
>
> * *The Internet Domain and Internet Protocol (IP) address from which you access our Web site;*
> * *The type of Internet browser and the operating system of the computer you use to access our site;*
> * *The date and time you visit our site;*

---

[83] NSA NSA is committed to protecting your privacy and will collect no personal information about you unless you choose to provide that information to us. Last visited 27.10.2013

- *The pages you visit on our site;*
- *If you linked to our Web site from another Web site, the address of that Web site;*
- *And, if you linked to our Web site from a search Web site, the address of the Web site and the search term you used.*

I do not understand this. They say that the information does not identify us personally, but they keep our internet protocol (IP) address. Isn't the IP address enough to identify us personally?

What if the Nobel Committee withdraws Barack Obama's Nobel Piece Price after the Snowdon scandal and the bugging of at least 35 other state leaders?

What if NSA had to stop their activities immediately?

What NSA could admit their activities and tell the people what's actually is going on?

They will not, their policy is; deny it and keep denying it and pretend it never happened.

What if people and business around the world start to lose faith in USA?

War

What if Hitler had not been born?

Adolf Hitler (1889-1945) was responsible for World War II; 100 million military personnel were mobilized, and around 60 million died.

What if Archduke Franz Ferdinand of Austria and his wife had not been shot dead in Sarajevo?

On 28 June 1914, Archduke Franz Ferdinand (1863-1914) and his wife were killed; the assassination triggered World War I. Would the war have started without the shooting?

What if Germany had not invaded Poland in September 1939?

The invasion triggered World War II.

What if the military never existed?

What if the Falklands War had not started?

What if the Battle of the Somme in France had never started?

The Battle of the Somme in 1916 was probably the most meaningless battle in history. The battle lasted for 140 days; more than one million soldiers lost their life, and it was the biggest man-made catastrophe. The battle probably cost $208,406,000,000 in addition to indirect costs like the cost of damaged buildings and loss of production of $40,000 trillion.

What if this amount had been spent on rebuilding the countries instead?

What if Hitler had finished his super cannon?

The plan was to bomb London from north France with a new super cannon, but it failed. Would the outcome of World War II have been different if Hitler had finished his dream?

What if the Cold War had never come to an end?

The Cold War (1946-1991) almost ended in a worldwide nuclear war during the Cuban Missile Crisis in 1962. President John F. Kennedy (1917-1963) and USSR Chairman Nikita Khrushchev (1894-1971) played a key role.

Wealth

What if you had one of the Bibles Gutenberg printed?

He printed 180 copies of the Bible; it is believed that there are only 21 left. Each of them would probably be worth $3 million.

What if you had bought shares in Diners Club in 1950?

You would definitely not need to use the very expensive credit card.

Weather

What if it starts snowing in the UK?

If there are two centimeters of snow in the UK, there is total chaos. The schools, airports, shops, offices, nursery schools, businesses, and everything closes. Beforehand, there are warnings of catastrophe on the radio, and people are told to buy food, medicine, blankets, and other necessities and stay indoors. How much does that cost businesses, the government, and individuals? At least, most people get an additional day off—maybe without being paid.

What if Heathrow Airport had to close due to snow for one week?

Heathrow Airport actually closed its runways on 18 December 2010, stranding hundreds of thousands of passengers, because its winter resilience contingency plan was only designed to keep the airport fully operational if less than an inch of snow fell. Britain's transport authorities knew the airport did not have the equipment, the manpower, or the crucial chemical deicers to cope with the six inches of snow that fell. The southern runway was shut for almost four days, leading to the cancellation of two thousand flights and huge delays for hundreds of others. Many flights were still being delayed or cancelled six days later.

The *Telegraph* investigation revealed that Heathrow[84]

- regarded more than two centimeters (0.8 inches) of continuous snow as blizzard conditions, grounds to suspend flight operations indefinitely,
- had only ten snow sweepers and three airfield de-icers available to clear the runways, despite publicly claiming it had sixty such vehicles,
- previously notified the government and the aviation authorities of its limited snow clearing capabilities,
- ruled out the Civil Aviation Authority's offer to relax its rules on runway clearance, which would have allowed planes to take off and land without clearing all the snow, and
- ordered in emergency supplies of runway de-icer because it had insufficient stocks to clear both runways.

This happened as thousands of travelers planned to go home or on holiday for Christmas. The closing of Heathrow cost individuals, businesses, and governments billions of pounds and caused wasted time for lots of people.

What if it happened again?

It will—next time it snows.

What if Heathrow Airport had to pay compensation to everyone for their losses?

They might have been bankrupt. They blamed the weather, but many delays and losses were due to bad management. They don't have compensation for delays due to bad weather, but they perhaps

---

[84] Lewis Jason. Heathrow bosses knew an inch of snow would cripple the airport. *The Telegraph*. 25 December 2010.

would have to pay compensation if the court agrees that all delays and losses are due to incompetent management. Next time, why not sue them?

What if we did not have weather forecasts or weather channels?

So what? They are always wrong anyway.

Work

What if you are in a middle of an interview for your dream job and have to go to the toilet?

What if you are making a speech in front of a large audience and open the speech with a loud fart?

What if nobody worked as a dentist?

What if nobody worked as a doctor?

What if nobody worked for the police?

What if nobody worked for the fire brigade?

What if nobody worked as a teacher?

What if nobody worked as a nurse?

What if nobody worked as a farmer?

What if nobody worked as a lawyer?

What if nobody worked as an engineer?

What if nobody worked as employees?

What if you could sack one person of your choice?

What if you were unemployed?

What if you had no income for three months?

What if you had no income for twelve months?

What if you had no bills for one year?

What if there were no labor or health and safety laws?

What would it be like to be an employee then?

What if your employer went bankrupt?

What if you could quit your job tomorrow?

Yes!

What if you could retire tomorrow?

What if nobody wasted office hours on the Internet?

How much time annually is spent on worthless e-mails, searching web pages, and being distracted by the web?

What if you could be your manager's boss?

What if you did not have any colleagues?

What if you over-slept on a day you have an important meeting or a job interview?

What if you could decide your own salary?

How much salary or what pay rise do you think you deserve?

What if there were no unions?

Some employers would probably be satisfied.

What if the president of the United States wanted to quit during the presidential term?

Would he be able to step down?

What if you had the worst job in the world and could not quit?

What is the world's worst job (except yours)?

What if no employees spent any time at all on private issues during working hours?

The companies would probably need significant fewer employees, and lots of people would be sacked. So is it good that employees spend time on private matters then?

What if you have another 'What if . . .' you might want to share with others?

Submit it on *www.whatif.uk.com* and it might be included in the next edition. You will find other what-ifs as well on this web page.

Bibliography

Adams, Charles. For Good and Evil: The Impact of Taxes on the Course of Civilization. Lanham, MD: Madison Books, 2011.

All Verdens Historie. 2011.

Black Richard. "Earth—melting in the heath?" BBC News Channel. 18 May 2007.

Cebula, Richard, and Edgar Feige. America's Underground Economy: Measuring the Size, Growth and Determinants of Income Tax Evasion in the US. 2011.

Control Risk and Simmons & Simmons. 2007.

Dagens Næringsliv. 2011, 2012.

Financial Times Global 500—based list is up to date as of March 28, 2013.

Friedlob, G. Thomas, and Franklin James Plewa. Understanding Balance Sheets. 1996.

Gaulin Grete. "Norges Mørke Historie" (Norways Dark History). Ny Tid, 8 May 2008.

Global Financial Integrity. 2011.

Illustrert Vitenskap Historie. 2006, 2012.

International Tax Review. 'Tax Evasion Clampdown Draws in € Billion, Says OECD.' 26 October 2011.

Lewis Jason. Heathrow bosses knew an inch of snow would cripple the airport. The Telegraph. 25 December 2010.

Lilico Andrew. "What happens when Greece defaults?" The Telegraph, 20 May 2011.

Moen Ole O. USAs Presidenter Fra George Washington til Barack Obama (USAs Presidents) 2009

NORAD 2009 report on tax havens and development.

Osman, Jenny. 100 Ideas that Changed the World. Our Most Important Discoveries Selected by Our Greatest Minds. 2011.

Patalon Bill. "What America's 2 Trillion Underground Economy Says About Jobs," Money Morning, 29 Apr. 2013.

Rabinowitz Marco. "Rise of the Shadow Economy: Second Largest Economy in the World". Forbes. 11 July 2011.

Schneider Friedrich, Svart økonomi har holdt Italia flytende (Shadow economy has kept Italy alive) E24.no, 9 Nov. 2011.

Sosabowski Dr. Hal. 100 Ideas that changed the world—Oxygen. The discovery of the gas of life.(2011).

Stengel, Richard. Time 100 Ideas that Changed the World. 2010.

Transparency International, GCB 2010.

Transparency International, TISDA.

United Nations Educational, Scientific, and Cultural Organization (UNESCO).

U.S. Cong., Senate, 39 Cong., 2nd Sess., "The Chivington Massacre," Reports of the Committees.

World Bank World Development Report. 2011.

Websites:

Adultlearn.com. http://www.filibustercartoons.com/monsters.htm.

Amnesty International. http://www.amnesty.org/en/who-we-are/about-amnesty-international.

Apple Annual Report 2012 http://www.sec.gov/Archives/edgar/data/320193/000119312512444068/d411355d10k.htm.

BBC News. http://www.bBC.co.uk/news/world-asia-pacific-13218733.

BBC News Channel. http://news.bBC.co.uk/1/hi/sci/tech/4315968.stm.

Brain Marshall. What would happened if the earth stood still for one full minute? HowStuffWorks. Inc. http://blogs.howstuffworks.com/2009/10/26/what-would-happen-if-the-earth-stood-still-for-one-full-minute/.

British Beer and Pub Association. http://www.beerandpub.com/index.aspx.

Butler Kiera. What would happen if an 8.9 quake hit the United States? Mother Jones and the Foundation for National Progress. http://www.motherjones.com/blue-marble/2011/03/what-would-happen-if-89-quake-hit-us.

Chan Casey. What would happen if every single person in the world pointed a laser pen at the moon? Gawker Media.http://gizmodo.com/5948820/what-would-happen-if-every-single-person-in-the-world-pointed-a-laser-pointer-at-the-moon.

Clark Josh. What if everybody in the United States flushed the toilet at the same time? HowStuffWorks. Inc. http://home.howstuffworks.com/home-improvement/plumbing/everybody-flushes-toilets.htm.

DNA of Cognac.' http://www.most-expensive-cognac.com/dna.php.

Edinformatics. http://www.edinformatics.com/inventions_inventors/.

Elistmania. http://www.elistmania.com/juice/the_10_deadliest_diseases/.

European Union. http://europa.eu/about-eu/basic-information/index_en.htm.

Famous Historical Events. http://www.famoushistoricalevents.net/.

Fraczek Witold. If the Earth Stood Still. Esri. Understanding the world. http://www.esri.com/news/arcuser/0610/nospin.html.

Gerbis Nicholas. What would happen if I drilled a tunnel through the centre of the earth and jumped into it? HowStuffWorks. Inc. http://science.howstuffworks.com/environmental/earth/geophysics/question373.htm.

Glenn. What would happen if you farted inside a space suit? Astonishing Science. Spectacular Museum. http://www.sciencemuseum.org.uk/onlinestuff/snot/what_would_happen_if_you_farted_in_a_space_suit.aspx.

Heimbuch Jaymi. What would happen if sharks disappeared? MNN Holding LLC. http://www.treehugger.com/ocean-conservation/what-would-happen-if-sharks-disappeared.html.

Hippokrates. The famous people. http://www.famoushistoricalevents. net/hippocratic-method/

How many people use the top social media, apps, and service," June 2013. http://expandedramblings.com/index.php/resource-how-many-people-use-the-top-social-media.

Intowine. http://www.intowine.com/what-cognac-history-most-famous-french-brandy.

Johannessen Ola. M. And what would happen if Gulf Stream stopped? Redrawn. http://ec.europa.eu/research/rtdinfo/special_pol/04/print_article_2603_en.html.

Limer Eric. What would happen if everyone on earth jumped at the same time? Gawker Media http://gizmodo.com/5936007/what-would-happen-if-everyone-on-earth-jumped-at-the-same-time.

McManis Ellen. What would happen if you tried to hit a baseball pitched at 90 per cent the speed of light? xkcd. http://what-if. xkcd.com/1/.

McNeil Michael. What if a rainstorm dropped all of its water in single giant drop? Xkcd. http://what-if.xkcd.com/12/.

Messmer Ellen. What if all law enforcement agencies could do instant DNA analysis? NetworkWorld Inc. http://www.networkworld. com/news/2012/100412-what-if-security-dna-262971.html.

NATO. http://www.nato.int/welcome/brochure_WhatIsNATO_en.pdf.

Neer Katherine. What would happen if the Hoover Dam broke? HowStuffWorks. Inc. http://science.howstuffworks.com/engineering/structural/hoover-dam-broke.htm.

Nestlé. http://www.nestle.com/AboutUs/KeyFigures/Pages/Key Figures.aspx.

Norsk Hydro. '1943: The Heroes from Telemark.' http://www. hydro.com/en/About-Hydro/Our-history/1929-1945/1943-The-Heroes-of-Telemark/.

O'Brian Derek. If my printer could literally print out money, would it have that big an effect on the world? Xkcd. http://what-if.xkcd. com/23/.

Odenwald Sten Dr. What would happen if the earth stopped spinning? Dr. Sten Odenwald. http://image.gsfc.nasa.gov/poetry/ask/q1168.html.

Olson Adrienne. If you went outside and lay down on your back with your mouth open, how long would you have to wait until a bird pooped in it? xkcd http://what-if.xkcd.com/11/.

O'Neil Brian. What would happen if a small black hole hit the earth? Universe Today. http://www.universetoday.com/12837/what-would-happen-if-a-small-black-hole-hit-the-earth/#ixzz295mY05St.

Rao Leena. What 20 Minutes On Facebook looks like. 31 Dec. 2010. http://techcrunch.com/2010/12/31/what-20-minutes-on-facebook-looks-like-1m-shared-links-2-7m-photos-uploaded-10-2m-comments/.

Sacom. Looking for Mickey Mouse's Conscience Campain. 11 Dec 2007. 12 Aug. 1013 last accessed.) http://www.evb.ch/cm_data/SACOM_Disney_report_11_12_07.pdf. Shine Conor.

Store Norske Leksikon. http://snl.no.

Strickland Jonathan. What would happen if the Internet collapsed? HowStuffWorks. Inc. http://computer.howstuffworks.com/internet/basics/internet-collapse.htm.

UN. http://www.un.org/en/aboutun/index.shtml.

The White House. http://www.whitehouse.gov/about/history/.

What could happen if Greece leaves the eurozone? BBC. http://www.bbc.co.uk/news/business-18074674.

What would happen if an earthquake struck Las Vegas? Las Vegas Sun. http://www.lasvegassun.com/news/2012/oct/03/city/.

What would happen if the entire world lived like Americans? The Change Generation. http://www.fastcoexist.com/1680379/what-would-happen-if-the-entire-world-lived-like-americans.

What would happen if a person with type B blood was given type O blood? Answer Corporation. http://wiki.answers.com/Q/What_would_happen_if_a_person_with_type_b_blood_were_given_type_o_blood

What would happen if type A blood were given to a person who has type B blood? Answer Corporation. http://wiki.answers. com/Q/What_would_happen_if_type_A_blood_was_given_ to_a_person_who_has_type_B_blood.

What would happen if type B blood were given to a person who has type A blood? Answer Corporation.http://wiki.answers. com/Q/What_would_happen_if_type_B_blood_was_given_ to_a_person_who_has_type_A_blood.

What would happen if the ozone layer was destroyed? Answer Corporation. http://wiki.answers.com/Q/What_would_happen_ if_the_Ozone_layer_was_destroyed.

What would happen if the United States went back to the gold standard? The Week Publications Inc. http://theweek.com/ article/index/232462/what-would-happen-if-the-us-went-back-to-the-gold-standard.

What would happen if you fired a gun on a train moving as fast as a bullet? HowStuffWorks. Inc. http://science.howstuffworks.com/ question456.htm.

What would happen if you lit 7000 wrapped sparklers? NatGeo TVUK. http://www.youtube.com/watch?v=t0H4GYxGx0Q.

What would happen if you peed on an electric fence? NatGeo TVUK. http://www.youtube.com/watch?v=t0H4GYxGx0Q&list =PLCE4262D88AB2C935.

What would happen if we don't recycle? Squidoo, LLC. http://www. squidoo.com/recycle-pollution.

What would happen if we stopped vaccinations? Centres for Disease Control and Prevention. http://www.cdc.gov/vaccines/ vac-gen/whatifstop.htm.

Wikipedia. http://en.wikipedia.org.

Wolchover Natalie. What would happen if a lion fought a tiger? Yahoo! Inc. http://news.yahoo.com/happen-lion-fought-tiger-112933787.html.

Wolchover Natalie. What would happen if you fell into a black hole? The Huffington Post. http://www.huffingtonpost.

com/2012/04/13/what-would-happen-if-you-fell-into-a-black-hole_n_1424517.html.

Wolchover Natalie. What would happen if you fell into a volcano? Discovery Communication LLC. http://news.discovery.com/earth/weather-extreme-events/volcano-garbage-waste-lava-burn-video-person-120627.htm.

Wolchover Natalie. What would happen if you shot a gun in space? TeckMedia Nework. http://www.livescience.com/18588-shoot-gun-space.html.